MARRIED
BUT NOT
ENGAGED

BOOKS BY
PAUL COUGHLIN

No More Christian Nice Guy
No More Christian Nice Guy Study Guide
Married . . . But Not Engaged (with Sandy Coughlin)

FROM THE AUTHOR OF NO MORE CHRISTIAN NICE GUY

PAUL & SANDY COUGHLIN

MARRIED
BUT NOT
ENGAGED

BETHANYHOUSE

MINNEAPOLIS, MINNESOTA

Published by Bethany House Publishers
11400 Hampshire Avenue South
Bloomington, Minnesota 55438

Bethany House Publishers is a division of
Baker Publishing Group, Grand Rapids, Michigan.

Printed in the United States of America

ISBN-13: 978-0-7642-0241-4
ISBN-10: 0-7642-0241-3

Library of Congress Cataloging-in-Publication Data

Coughlin, Paul T.
    Married—but not engaged : why men check out and what you can do to create the intimacy you desire / Paul and Sandy Coughlin.
        p. cm.
    Summary: "The authors, a married couple, help women realize relief from false guilt and shame and show them how to engage their 'checked out' husbands with wisdom, grace, and love"—provided by publisher.
    ISBN 0-7642-0241-3 (hardcover : alk. paper)
    1. Marriage—Religious aspects—Christianity. 2. Husbands—Psychology.
3. Men—Psychology. I. Coughlin, Sandy. II. Title.
    BV835.C685   2006
    248.8'44—dc22   2006013678

We dedicate this book
to the power of love, friendship,
and intimacy—all gifts from God.

ABOUT THE AUTHORS

PAUL COUGHLIN, author of *No More Christian Nice Guy*, hosts a radio talk show on The Dove in southern Oregon. He has been interviewed by C-SPAN, the *New York Times*, and numerous radio and television stations. His articles have appeared in *New Man, Faithworks, Ministries Today, Today's Christian Woman,* and other periodicals. He is a contributing writer for Crosswalk.com, the world's largest Christian Web site. A former Christian Nice Guy, Paul is a passionate husband to Sandy and enthusiastic father to three active children. He loves jazz, soccer, cycling, fly-fishing, gardening, and photography, and hates playing Scrabble.

SANDY COUGHLIN works from home and is active in her local public schools and community where she serves in multiple volunteer roles, including PTO advisor. Sandy is a passionate wife to Paul and enthusiastic mother to two handsome sons and one lovely daughter. She loves running, hosting parties, cooking, ballroom dancing with her husband, and playing Scrabble. The Coughlin family lives in Oregon.

ACKNOWLEDGMENTS

Thanks to Sandy's running partners: Jenny, Kristi, Carrie, and Pam. Our 5:00 a.m. runs were more than exercise. We covered love, relationships, and life.

Thanks Ted, Bill, and Kelly for sharing our travels on the road toward intimacy.

Barb Wiedenbeck for your insight, encouragement, research, and lamb.

Bill and Dee Strock and Minor and Jeannie Matthews who are examples of long-lasting, engaging marriages.

Hoppi Lilien, who provided Thursday night gourmet meals and love to our family.

Finally, thank you to the hundreds of people who shared their struggles and success in understanding and overcoming the Nice Guy problem in their marriage. You have shown great courage and faith.

"Taste and see that the Lord is *good*."
Psalm 34:8 (emphasis added)

TABLE OF CONTENTS

I'm the woman who married Paul, a man who struggled hard against being a Christian Nice Guy. After he wrote a book about it—*No More Christian Nice Guy*—we received a lot of letters. Most fall into the "Thank you for changing my life" category.

Then there's another category: "Thank you . . . but . . ." These come from the wives of Christian Nice Guys who still want desperately to be closer to their husbands, the men they thought they knew when they married them but to whom they found another side soon thereafter. A frequently difficult, sometimes maddening, and regularly frustrating side. Most continue to love, but their love is growing thin. Some admit they aren't sure if they do love their man anymore, given all the destruction he's wrought, and part of that because of his passive ways. These women want help sorting out their confusion and pain.

Sister in turmoil, I have been in your uncomfortable high heels. My husband didn't struggle alone with this problem. I struggled as well, and so did our marriage. That's why Paul and I have written this book together, to help you learn from our victories and mistakes along the road toward intimacy.

Maybe you're wondering how you can regain respect for a man who is consistently passive, frequently fearful, habitually resistant to committing or even making decisions. Wishy-washy . . . won't shoot straight with his boss . . . won't stand up to his parents . . . placates rather than connects with his kids . . . highly values looking good in the eyes of others . . . can't say no to volunteer opportunities or church obligations . . . often puts you last.

Rigidity—a silent, insidious intimacy killer—has set into your marriage. Your battle lines are poured and set in concrete; somehow you're either becoming or have become a desperate housewife, except this isn't a TV show, and nothing's funny anymore.

Your marriage isn't turning out like the ones you saw (or thought you saw) in church. This isn't the life you envisioned or planned for as a younger woman. You struggle with resentment, perhaps bitterness, perhaps shame.

You're married to a CNG. A *Christian Nice Guy.*

So was I. I was almost twenty-eight when Paul and I married, and I saw amazing qualities in him. His charm, intelligence, and humor were enough for me to never look back. His gifts and abilities were always there, and I never doubted them. I knew God had a powerful future for his life—I *knew* God had given him talents and a significant purpose. I believed in my husband!

But I didn't want to run the show; in no sphere is marriage meant to be a one-person undertaking. Sure, I could manage the household, pay the bills, plan the events, and as Paul says, teach assertiveness training classes. At the same time, in every sense, in every way, I wanted us to be in it together—to be connected, to be joined, to be cooperative . . . to be *engaged*.

It's one thing to have different roles and differing responsibilities; it's another to live, metaphorically but functionally, in different worlds. Generally, whenever one spouse's emotions (feelings) and will (choices) are disengaged, troubles follow. Specifically, though, when you combine a passive guy and an assertive gal, there will be far more than underwear to pick up and dishes to wash. You'll also have a build-up of anger or rage to disinfect, a diminished or dissolving intimacy to cleanse and restore, a loss of trust and respect to reestablish and renew. And much more.

Frustration set in for me when I couldn't fathom why Paul wouldn't stand up for himself at work. *Do I need to call his boss and take care of business myself?* I wondered. *Where is his courage, his willpower? Why is he silent with me? Why won't he make his needs known? Why does he have this need to please?* And, for me, the worst question of all: *Why am I walking on eggshells?*

I didn't know what a "Christian Nice Guy" was—I thought all Christian men were nice guys! After all, that's what I learned in church; that's either what they were or what they were supposed to be. I saw men with smiles on their faces. Men who were mellow, men who didn't fight or argue or confront. Men who regarded "turning the other cheek" as synonymous with not expressing anger, or any such "negative" emotion, at least where others could see or hear it.

For years I heard from the pulpit how meek and mild Jesus was. I can't ever think of a time that I heard my pastor speak of Christ's boldness, aside from turning over the tables in the temple, or God's having wrath upon us for not doing this or that (rules and regulations). When Paul and I married, I got exactly what I expected from my husband: a nice Christian guy.

Fortunately, God intervened in our life in two ways. He got hold of Paul. Then, in an unexpected maneuver, he got hold of me. I learned that my responses, though normal, were part of the problem too. Oh, my aching pride!

He began to change me, teaching me to be more supportive and to place more trust in my husband. My respect for Paul was strengthened as I became able to see his struggles in a healthier light. My respect was enhanced even more when Paul started being more open and honest, when he began to exert his will and express his feelings. I listened to him more, prayed for him more, and was warmer toward him in general. We began to lean toward each other. We were building intimacy.

We hope *Married . . . But Not Engaged* brings you hope, encouragement, and insight as you embark on the quest to create or rediscover genuine intimacy in your marriage (or marriage-to-be). Every woman wants her man to be "engaged," and not in the sense of putting a ring on her finger, but in terms of being emotionally present. How you relate to him and interact with him can make an incredible difference; you don't have to stand by and watch your marriage slip away, and you don't have to nag, coerce, and push away your Nice Guy.

In the following chapters, from a former CNG's perspective, Paul will share what causes a man's passivity, what destruction takes place when a man decides to be nice instead of good, and what you can do to help your man find and use his emotional compass. I'll share ways I tried to foster and facilitate change, including why most of my attempts didn't work, and what ultimately proved to restore to our marriage the intimacy we both wanted.

CHAPTER 1

IT DOESN'T HAVE TO BE THIS WAY

A complaint is an intimate moment in disguise.

DR. PAUL COLEMAN

Sometimes they shake Paul's hand and have a hard time letting go. Some give him the preacher's handshake and grab his elbow too. Though their grip may change, their eye contact is surprisingly similar and noticeably intense, and their questions are always about the same gender.

This is what happens when Paul tells women what he does: he helps men, especially Christian men, overcome passivity and the damage it creates. He shares his testimony:

> I used to think it was wrong and sinful to express what I really thought, to exert my will. For years I lived out a dangerous caricature of "gentle Jesus, meek and mild" that made life, especially marriage, boring and dreadful.

These women, whose goodwill Paul respects and admires, say, "You just described my brother . . . son . . . boyfriend . . . grandson." But by far, the noun accompanied by the most emotion is *husband*; for these women, intimacy is like a beautiful dress in a magazine: something they hope for and dream about but wonder if they'll ever have. Their husbands are married but not *engaged*.

Even the fact that Paul gives their nebulous misery a name, the Christian Nice Guy problem, provides relief. What Paul teaches brings clarity to what for so long was an obscure and dark presence in their soul and in their marriage. It helps them see how their intuition is confirming something real and profound about what's really happening (*I don't know why, but he's not telling me the truth, he's avoiding me and others, he's hiding from life*) even while their husbands tell them not to worry, that everything's great.

Paul received this note from a CNG wife:

> Your book *No More Christian Nice Guy* describes my husband to a T. He's the great pretender. He wants people to think that his life is great when it's not. But others don't see it because he's so "nice" to everyone. He's nasty behind the scenes and I walk on eggshells. I wonder sometimes if I'm losing my mind.

Another writes:

> When we were presenters during the Marriage Encounter getaway weekend, my husband identified the "mask" he wears most as Mr. Nice Guy. When he took the quiz on your Web site, he answered yes to nearly every question. He has said that he wants to be a Good Guy, to use your label, versus [being] a Nice Guy.
>
> Somewhere along the way [in his life], he decided that anger and conflict must be avoided at all costs. So he (similar to his mom) became a great pretender and avoider, focusing on whether or not his life looked good regardless of whether it truly was good. Our

finances are in a huge state of crisis. He's been unfaithful, which was devastating to our marriage. What a crazy cycle, and I'm trying to see the big picture and live as healthy as I can, realizing I can't control what my husband does or doesn't do, or even what he believes or understands.

Here's a common scenario for the CNG wife: the guy she fell in love with and married, who she now struggles to understand, respect, and even like, is low-voltage (until he has a sudden surge or anger overload), a sideline husband/father. He's easygoing (until he explodes), and he goes out of his way to never ruffle feathers—even when he should. Like mascara, he runs when deeper emotions are expressed. He's a Nice Guy, so he smiles, but you can tell his expression is not born from peace, contentment, or happiness. Like a baby smiling from gas pain, Christian Nice Guys smile in response to something that bothers their stomach: fear, anxiety, and the terror of encountering conflict.

The following test will help you discern if your marriage is infected by CNG-ness. If you answer yes to two or more questions in each category, he's seriously into being nice instead of good (to the detriment of your marriage). One yes in each category still spells marital trouble. Five yeses overall means his "nice" tendencies make marital intimacy difficult to obtain and maintain.

Any of these three results means this book is definitely for you.

Nice Guy or Good Guy?

Faith Life:

- Does he dismiss, or never discuss, Gospel passages where Jesus isn't nice?
- When pondering "WWJD," does he assume a gentle response?
- Does he think conflict and anger are sins?

- Is he the guy at church who never says no to an assignment?
- Does he think being a Christian is about being pleasant, showing impeccable manners, and subjecting himself to the will of others?
- Do you feel he uses Christianity as a way to hide from life?

Home Life:

- Does he have a relational history in which he's tried to rescue troubled women?
- Does he lack leadership in your family?
- Does he make you the emotional center of his life?
- If he is regularly unclear about his sexual desires, does he become angry, sullen, or give you the silent treatment when they go unmet?
- Does he have a hard time standing up to his mother?
- Do you resent how his passivity influences your life?
- Is he hard to respect because he appears weak?
- Does he avoid setting (let alone achieving) goals?
- Does he seem directionless to the point where you have begun to question whether you have direction as well?

Work Life:

- Does he say one thing to one person but something different to another?
- Does he smile, even when he doesn't like what's happening to him, and then rant about it later?
- Does he hide his mistakes, even when there are few or no consequences?
- Does he find himself working for abusive bosses?
- Does he make less money than you know he should?

Life in General:

- Does he feel embarrassed when people compliment him?

- Does he inspire in you a dissatisfying level of romantic interest?
- Does he think it's selfish to have normal wants and desires?
- Does he think that avoiding conflict will improve his life?
- If someone is angry with him, does he automatically think he's wrong?
- Does he hide his flaws, even from people he trusts?
- Does he usually analyze life instead of feeling life?
- Does he live as if feelings are a waste of time even for "weaker" people?
- Does fear often keep him immobile and indecisive?
- Does he rage or abuse in ways that just don't make sense to you?

Diagnosing a CNG Marriage

In the wacky world of niceness, the vices of fear and passivity masquerade as virtues. Paul and I didn't even know our marriage was stuck there until God's fantastic grace helped us realize it. Help is on the way for you; please keep reading. This book is meant to bring you hope and be a salve of healing for your careworn heart.

At one time I (Sandy) answered yes to some of those questions, and when it comes to marriage and the Christian Nice Guy issue, we've had three unforgettable teachers: Professors Pain, Suffering, and Misery. Thank God we dealt with them before they gained tenure. We want to encourage you and show you how to do the same.

For you who say "My husband's a nice guy, but . . .": *Married . . . But Not Engaged* gets to the heart of the matter, explaining what intimacy is (and isn't), why it's missing, what happens when it's absent, where his seemingly inexplicable behavior comes from, and what can be done to bring change and growth.

None of the many books about creating greater intimacy exposes Nice Guy wedded woes like this one. Recognizing and facing falsehoods about men—about masculinity—is a crucial piece of the information you need to graft increased insight and wisdom into your marriage. This may be part of why other messages about intimacy haven't worked or haven't changed your relationship: they didn't substantially address this perplexing matter that influences countless (and especially Christian) marriages.

If what you've read so far describes your struggle with real intimacy, then deep inside you also know that you stand on shaky ground. You just don't respect your husband the way you want to, and you're pretty sure he's not being straightforward and truthful, but his words are so nuanced that he's never caught red-handed. He hides from emotions, and he's terrified of criticism. Your heart is growing or has grown cold toward the man you once found desirable and captivating but now find frustrating and flat. If your coldness reaches an advanced stage, your heart will begin to wander.

ISN'T *NICE* WHAT THE CHURCH HAS TAUGHT MEN TO BE?

One of Sandy's friends had left her CNG. "*Why* did she leave?" I (Paul) asked, when talking with Sandy and another woman. Immediately they replied, nearly in unison, "Because he was too nice." Five potent words bore the crux of the issue into me more deeply than any sermon on marriage in memory.

"Too nice!" I yelled. "Isn't that what the church has taught men to be?!"

He *was* nice—nicest person you could meet. But if you were in his home, you'd notice that he wasn't all there. If he were a photo, he'd be both background and foreground. His personality lacked distinguishing edges and features because, tragically, he'd cleared his life of them in trying to become the "ideal Christian man." If he had an opinion, he kept it to himself. He seemed incapable of expressing difficult or heavy emotions. Conversation was light, always breezy and on the safe side.

Like most CNGs, he was a man in search of a personality: pleasantly evasive. He used all his energy on keeping up appearances. His seemingly contrived smile wouldn't go away. He followed a rigid life-script, and he showed no vitality. You'd leave his company drained, fatigued, knowing that you'd just spent time with someone you didn't know and couldn't know. Sadly, his wife apparently felt the same way.

The fear in a Nice Guy's heart makes it impossible for him to achieve the abundant life Jesus came to give but warned is hard to find. Fear prevents loving another person and truly accepting love in return. Fear, the archenemy of all CNGs, keeps intimacy at arm's length.

Sometimes, before your own eyes, you find you're becoming a Mrs. Christian Nice Lady. Seeking to keep the peace, you take on the same dishonest pose. But inside, you know this is peace-faking, not peace-making. Your troubled soul reminds you, adding to the already present anxiety of tiptoeing around the issues and staying parted from the facts. Please be assured: You are not powerless, you are not alone, and you can make a phenomenal difference.

Some stereotypes—pointedly, stereotypes about domineering or controlling wives—might suggest that the women who hold on when they shake my hand *want* their husbands pliable and agreeable. The opposite is true. "I wish he would tell me what he really thinks—even if it bothers me," says one. "I wish he would stand up to me and say no sometimes," says another. "I can't get my husband to express *any* feelings," a third bemoans. To one sitting next to me on a plane, who stated that she walks on eggshells but doesn't really know why, I said, to her surprise, "Sandy used to say the same thing."

All these women, young and old, want to know, *"What can I do?"* While their love for a troubled man is touching, the state of their sour marriages is alarming. They confess their constant confusion and increasing indifference. Some just want to hide. Many have difficulty sleeping. Their world has lost its color and its depth.

Here's what they need to know: They can help their man transform from a shut-down and unreliable Christian Nice Guy into a loving, protective, and passionate Christian Good Guy. A man with such opportunity is in a good place, for he has yet to chew through all of his wife's goodwill. Though the clock is ticking, there's still time.

Just as important as what these women *can* do is what they *shouldn't* do. For many, it's what they're doing now: begging, pushing, pleading, nagging, yelling, even hitting their CNG. Some shoulder the bazooka of shame, line him up in their sites, and fire away. Understandable, since nothing else seems to get his attention, but still destructive and always off limits.

One Direction or the Other

Intimacy, respect, and related blessings either grow or shrivel. They are fed, or they starve. The human heart grows heavier when burdened with the excruciating emotions and elements common to CNG marriages.

The Christian Nice Guy problem is all about shrinkage, all about hunger. The chapters ahead show what needs to happen to create new growth and the challenges this growth requires. We'll share our hearts as we confess our doubts, sins, misconceptions, mistakes, and (thank you, God!) breakthroughs. You'll read about others embarking on this endeavor as well. You'll see what happens when CNG burdens are lifted. You'll see freedom reign as new passions bloom all around it.

Finally, we hope you see that much of the problem likely isn't about you, and that no guy wants a CNG marriage. Trust us on this—the mess it creates isn't intentional. We want its underlying factors and roots, until now perhaps undetected, to come into view, bringing you solid hope and a reason to give your tense world the biggest sigh of relief you've ever had.

An important distinction: This book is written for marriages touched by the problem of *passive* husbands. Though such men can also exhibit *passive-aggressive* characteristics, they are typically not as abusive or flat-out dangerous. Passive-aggressive men are deliberately deceptive; passive men tend to be deceptive at the moment, not usually as premeditated.

Passive-aggressive men see relationships as primarily a struggle for power, and they believe for similar reasons that they can't be honest about their normal wants and needs, instead resorting to manipulation. Though CNG marriages have struggles for power, their issues aren't as intense and replete with dishonesty.

Passive and passive-aggressive men don't fit neatly into one camp or the other, and one of the biggest areas of overlap is that both fear intimacy. Perhaps one significant difference is that the passive-aggressive personality fights back more, and fights dishonestly; while both are controlled by fear, the passive-aggressive husband responds with more rage and more guile.

Scott Wetzler, PhD, describes such men:

> The truth is that the passive-aggressive man doesn't ride an emotional seesaw (although he may put you on one); he's not passive today and aggressive tomorrow, depending on the circumstances. Rather, the passive-aggressive man is simultaneously passive and aggressive. The paradox reigns because he *renounces his aggression as it is happening.*[1]

Though Wetzler does not explore in great depth the profound religious component of the Nice Guy problem (some passive and passive-aggressive men are masters at twisting the Bible to distance themselves from legitimate scrutiny), his *Living With the Passive-Aggressive Man* will help you comprehend other components of this issue and understand more about passive and passive-aggressive traits and behaviors.

We want to thank Dr. Paul Coleman for his excellent work, *The Complete Idiot's Guide to Intimacy*,[2] which explains the mystery and misconceptions surrounding intimacy, a vital component to lasting love. We also express sincere gratitude to Dan Allender and Tremper Longman III for writing *The Intimate Mystery: Creating Strength and Beauty in Your Marriage*.[3]

Now: It's time to consider the inner workings of that man of yours.

CHAPTER 2

THREE FORCES THAT MAKE (AND KEEP) MEN PASSIVE

The ordinary man is passive.... Against major events
he is as helpless as against the elements. So far from
endeavoring to influence the future, he simply
lies down and lets things happen to him.[1]

GEORGE ORWELL

Somewhere, a passive man is putting down his sword, changing his destiny and the destiny of his wife and children. It's taking place right now across the land. The first chapter of a faulty life-script is being scribbled at this moment.

Another man is already there—the rejection of his identity and the relinquishment of his essence happened when he was a boy. Something broke him, disoriented him, shamed him, and compelled him to surrender his own will—that extension of his inner person to the world outside him. Without fanfare he slid under life's radar and resigned himself to a cold fate.

If only we could see these figurative Nice Guy swords laying around us. We would find them tarnished on playgrounds, in classrooms, on kitchen floors. We would trip over them in backyards, sit on them in backseats. College dorms have a sword-pile by the Dumpster. Swords cover the hard-packed ground of coal mines, litter the hardwood floors of boardrooms, and clutter the bedrooms of family homes.

A man who has lost his masculinity feels like he has lost his virginity without wanting to. He crawls into his dark cave to hide, to heal; he may cover himself with a blanket of fantasy and try to escape entirely from the real. A die has been cast. All manner of assumptions and conclusions are drafted within the confines of his troubled mind. Fears fester and then foster lies, falsehoods about who he is and what life is really about. He becomes deceived, disillusioned, and dysfunctional.

> **THE PASSIVE MAN IS LIKE A SOLDIER WHO WAS NEVER TOLD THE WAR IS OVER. HE REMAINS ON GUARD AGAINST A FOE WHO ISN'T THERE.**

He probably doesn't talk about or officially sanction the major tenets of his belief system, three of which are fear, anger, and resentment. But this framework is there, ever-present, guiding his steps and dictating his decisions. He doesn't know that it's keeping him from love and life, but it is.

The casts on the broken bones of his thoughts and feelings were necessary for protection during healing, but he didn't heal, and he isn't healing, and now his muscles have atrophied; his growth is stunted. His self-preservation took over and never let go. Now an adult, he's like a soldier who was never told the war is over. He remains on guard against a foe who isn't there.

Before we get into the common sources of passivity in today's man—and Christian men in particular—we need a more accurate understanding of what it means to be passive.

In the dictionary sense, passivity is defined as the quality of being passive, which means someone tends to obey without questioning or resisting; to respond, rather than initiate; to submit to outside forces. When applied to the Nice Guy problem, passivity is better understood as *possessing a perilously limited will,* which leaves a man, his wife, and his children open to many forms of abuse and manipulation, often leading to anger and resentment. Will—choice, determination, volition—should be utilized to guide, to determine, to provide, to defend. However, a passive man turns his will inward, earmarking most or all of his energy to protect himself. For reasons that will soon be more apparent, your CNG thinks it's wrong to exert himself, to express a range of emotions, and to live like the real Jesus.

Force #1: A Culture at Odds With Masculinity

We could devote an entire book to examples of how our culture is confused (at best) about what a man is and vilifies (at worst) what it does know. One of the best examples is from the dictionary; compare the following.

Masculinity, 1905: Having the qualities of a man; virile, not feminine or effeminate; strong; robust. (Note: the word *effeminate* was once considered to be synonymous with *nice*.)[2]

Masculinity, 2005: The state of being a man or boy; those qualities conventionally supposed to make a man a typical or excellent specimen of manhood, traditionally physical strength and courage.

Painful to witness. Note the qualifying words *conventionally, supposed,* and *traditionally* in today's definition. Our dictionary, a definer of words, can't even take a definitive stand on masculinity and what it represents.

A study that compared gender stereotypes common in the 1970s to those widespread in the 1990s found that while views of women have improved, views of men have plummeted. Women are characterized as "intelligent, logical, independent, adventurous, dependable, skilled at relationships." Men? "Jealous, moody, fussy, temperamental, deceptive, narrow-minded, heedless of consequences." The report characterized this view of men as "negative masculinity."[3]

Imagine if someone marketed a line of clothing imprinted with "Girls Are Stupid. Throw Rocks at Them." Imagine the storm of protest if shirts and pajamas said, "Cats Are Stupid. Throw Rocks at Them." CNN and the *New York Times* would be camped out on the designer's and/or the retailers' doorsteps, demanding an interview and denouncing the brand in their editorials.

But no such outcry has yet taken place in response to the work of Todd Goldman, who estimated he would make $100 million in 2005 for his clothing line that touts, "Boys Are Stupid. Throw Rocks at Them," "Boys Are Smelly," and "Boys Are Pigs." "I'm all about in-your-face irreverence," he states.[4] He might also have added prejudice.

The Essence of the Culture's Message

What's the primary premise behind our society's denigration of males? Why do so few find it wrong and unacceptable to demoralize men? The root idea: *Men are a serious problem that must be fixed, not a gender to be appreciated. Men are not okay as men. Masculinity, in and of itself, is negative.*

We as a culture have undergone extended therapy at the hands of social engineers, media presentations, and dedicated activists. The script men and women followed before the social revolutions of the '60s and '70s was flawed; however, rather than addressing the flaws in order to right them, much of society began instead to reverse or invert the flaws. Human value and dignity is about all people being of equal worth; we needed to embrace and enact positive change in the ways women were viewed and treated, not say, "Men have had the upper hand and abused it; now it's women's turn to rule and degrade."

We're constantly told that not only is gender pliable and culturally orchestrated but also that the base nature or essence that men do manage to retain is harmful and wrong. The message has been clear: Men are what's wrong with the world. Even conservatives like George Gilder (in his pivotal work *Men and Marriage*) have repeated this myth, though in a more nuanced way.

We are still digging out from under the rubble of this societal experiment gone awry. For our purposes now, here's the point: That man of yours still doesn't know who he is and how he should behave. He has inherited a legacy of shame for being male; he rejects his true nature, his actual identity, and hides what's left of himself from others.

The Disposable Man

The most shaming and heartbreaking message is that a man is disposable. Maureen Dowd's *Are Men Necessary?* would be humorous if it weren't for her deadly serious attack upon manhood. The main thesis of Peggy Drexler and Linden Gross's *Raising Boys Without Men* is that boys are best raised by women; not only are fathers expendable, they're detrimental to the rearing of boys. TV sitcoms have perfected the image of men as naturally incompetent husbands and fathers, buffoons either to be set straight or cast aside.

Men have spiraled into "bewildered and lonely creatures," writes Professor Lionel Tiger, author of *The Decline of Males*. Why? They have been increasingly marginalized from one of life's most precious decisions: fatherhood. "Contraceptive technology [increasingly] controlled by women" has made a growing number of men feel obsolete, "resulting in their unprecedented withdrawal from family systems."[5]

When men have been allowed to be more involved in the creation of children, they've sometimes been told that nothing is needed but their sperm—that their love and time and guidance are superfluous. In the last decade, this destructive belief led to the derogatory expression "Sperm Donors." (Imagine the uproar if men referred to women as mere "Breeders.") This is the verdict rendered to men: "You're not needed for the creation and raising of a family." Men have responded by living down to this dismissive insult.

By contrast, the record shows how essential men are to children and to society in general.[6] The largest predictive factor in whether a child will graduate from high school, attend college, avoid crime, reject drugs, or become an unwed parent before eighteen is the presence of a father in the child's life. According to a recent Health and Human Services report, "Fathers play a unique role in fostering the well-being of their children, not only through providership, protection and guidance, but also through the way that they nurture the next generation."[7]

Yet there's a huge catch: "A father's involvement with his children . . . is powerfully contingent on the mother's attitude" toward him.[8] Research on children consistently indicates that the father-child relationship depends more on the quality of the parents' relationship than does the mother-child relationship. See the catch? Women have been told (by Gloria Steinem) that they need a man "like fish need bicycles"; for decades, women have been encouraged to deny children an influence more beneficial than good nutrition. The facts show that this low view of men hurts children, and the societal damage has been unprecedented. The radical feminism that wants to eliminate masculinity darkens the future for kids, especially boys.

The same report makes it even clearer:

> Girls with active dads demonstrate higher levels of mathematical competence, and boys with more nurturing fathers display higher levels of verbal acumen. It is worth noting, of course, that girls tend to struggle more with math and boys tend to struggle more with language. Having an active, emotionally invested father appears to help children overcome the intellectual weaknesses typically associated with their sex. . . .
>
> Fathers are more likely to foster independent, exploratory behavior on the part of their children, compared to mothers. . . . Children raised by engaged fathers are more comfortable exploring the world around them. . . . A playful, challenging, and nurturing approach to fatherhood is associated with more self-control and pro-social behavior among children throughout the course of their lives. . . .
>
> One study of seventh graders found that boys who had close relationships with their fathers were more likely to control their feelings and impulses, to obey rules at school and home, and to make good moral judgments. . . . This same study found that boys with involved fathers had fewer school behavior problems and that girls had more self-esteem. . . .
>
> Boys and girls who are exposed to the nurture of a father, and to see a father being nurturing to their mother and other adults, are much less likely to associate masculinity with predatory sexual behavior and hyper-aggressiveness. . . . Fathers help their children— especially their daughters—develop the self-control and the sense of self-worth that protects them from premature sexual intercourse and teenage pregnancy.[9]

When a man does not feel needed, something in him dies. Even an emotionally healthy man turns passive and loses energy. More so for a Nice Guy. This is why telling men that they are disposable is more than harmful. It's evil. If you want to motivate your Nice Guy, help him feel needed, not disposable.

The day before our wedding Paul's VW started leaking gas. Rotten gas line. He needed help fixing it in short time. Paul was reluctant to ask his father for help because he didn't want to ask him to do manual labor during such an important visit. But his dad jumped at the opportunity. It was one the best two-hour time frames in their lives. Though they smelled like gas and grease afterward, Paul's dad glowed from the realization that his son still needed him. Men come alive when they feel like your life is better with them. It makes them feel heroic.

We know that it's hard to keep him bolstered this way, even in the best of marriages. John Gray, author of one of the bestselling books on relationships, *Men Are From Mars, Women Are From Venus,*[10] explains how women during dating speak the following unspoken lauguage loud and clear. "We need you. Your power and strength can bring us great fulfillment, filling a void deep within our being. Together we could live in great happiness."

This unspoken message motivated their man to become larger and more attractive during dating. But after marriage, the usual challenges set in, made worse by Nice Guy tendencies to avoid conflict, which to their wives appears like they're trying to avoid responsibilities. This is true, though it is not their original motivation. He no longer feels wanted. He feels like a big fat problem. He may feel this way because he's been told so.

Force #2: The Psychology of Passivity

Given our cultural predicament, the Nice Guy disease affects every man differently, worse for some than for others. Some men are more predisposed to passive thought and behavior, and it's not rocket science figuring out why. Their lives are over-influenced by fear and related emotions like anxiety, which seal up the heart and prevent the sharing of emotions and the interchange of love. The usual suspects for this psychological tendency include childhood abuse, neglect, and abandonment.

Tom Cruise battled the effects of childhood abuse and bullies at school. He says his father, Thomas Cruise Mapather III, "was a bully and a coward . . . the kind of person who, if something goes wrong, they kick you. It was a great lesson in my life—how he'd lull you in, make you feel safe, and then, *bang!* Cruise struggled with anxiety not only from not trusting his own father at a young age but also from what happened at school: "So many times the big bully comes up, pushes you. Your heart's pounding, you sweat, and you feel like you're going to vomit . . . I don't like bullies."[11]

If passivity haunts your man, know that he *wasn't* "born this way." It's not his natural personality type, and it shouldn't be mistaken for being reserved. A *reserved* man may take longer than others to share his feelings, make decisions, and engage socially, but in the end he does express himself, make his will known, and connect with others. Though he's cautious, he still proceeds. A *passive* man, fear-frozen, is (and sees himself as) acted upon, rather than actively participating in life.

I (Paul) want to tell you part of my story. My childhood was a confusing mixture of love and abuse. I was physically, emotionally, and mentally battered

THIS IS IMPORTANT: THE PASSIVE MAN WAS *NOT* "BORN THIS WAY."

by my overwhelmed and troubled mother, who herself was battered by a troubled father.

We were created in the image of God, and we aren't robots, though we sometimes wish we were, so we could avoid emotional suffering. We *will* react to such treatment because God made us to feel. The question is, how?

All people respond to the pain of their past. Some learn to acknowledge and handle it in healthy ways. Some hold on to it, become passive, and join Victim Nation, blaming others for their destructive behavior as they use and abuse. Some come out of the gate swinging, becoming aggressive and making an unofficial allegiance with themselves: *I'm so determined that no one is ever going to abuse me again that I'm going on the offensive, making sure to get them before they get me.*

Nice Guys? They say (and may come to believe) that nothing really bad has ever happened. They deny their pain and its sources. They become masters of pretense, so intent on avoiding life and facing issues that they will create a fantasy world within and around themselves to escape.

Dr. Laura—no cream puff when it comes to taking responsibility for your life—writes in *Bad Childhood—Good Life,* "Many people don't even realize that their childhood history *has* impacted their adult thought and behavioral patterns in unproductive ways. . . . They don't realize that much of their adult life has been dedicated to repeating ugly childhood dynamics. . . . They're reduced to believing that neither they nor life matters much anyway, not understanding that they have the power and the choice to make a good life."[12] Not only do Nice Guys have the power of choice at their disposal, but they also must acknowledge their responsibility to become a redemptive force to transform what was meant for evil and make it good instead.

I (Paul) used to talk about the ideality of my childhood, but when a counselor finally probed deeper and I opened up, I began to recount repeated, profound abuse and humiliation. *No More Christian Nice Guy* recounts this at greater length; the following is a summary.

> My mother hit, slapped, and battered me more times than I can remember. She received a special rush of supremacy when she did so in public. She was indignant if I dared to defend myself, so I learned to relax, to roll with the blows much like a stuntman. This way the beatings were shorter; more intense, but shorter.
>
> The best way to describe what it felt like is through the events of

the film *Saving Private Ryan,* especially the beginning, when Allied soldiers storm the beaches of Normandy. The camera shakes violently, as I was shaken violently—there was no stopping the attack. Soldiers drown in the tidal waters, as I drowned emotionally on land. The thunderclaps of battle make young men lose their minds, as the verbal assault scattered my thoughts as well. Terror has them in its grip, reducing them, and reducing me, to human rubble. . . .

Among the most frightening moments in my life came when I returned home from elementary school. Mother, prone to emotional meltdowns, would stand on the front porch, cigarette in her right hand, left hand clutching the black iron railing. She was a human gate who stood tall for a short woman, electrified by a perverse power. The look in her eyes was the same as on the men who beat Jesus in *The Passion of the Christ* . . . sadistic pleasure. *See what I get to do to you today,* it guaranteed. The first blow sometimes landed before I could scramble through the door. I found myself face down many times. I still remember the metallic taste of blood. . . .

Other days when I'd find her in the same place (the porch) with the same intimidating position, I couldn't tell from her indifferent expression what she was going to do next. Her hugs and her hits came from the same baffling source. I entered my home the way a marine enters buildings in a war zone: tentatively, and with pounding heart. No wonder I didn't do much homework; I had survival on my mind.

It may sound weird, but you get used to physical beatings—like meals, they become part of your "normal" day. Though it's unpredictable knowing when they will begin, they take on a familiar pattern once they commence. You try to shut down your emotions the best you can and simply absorb the onslaught. The first blows are the worst; then your attacker fatigues. (Thank God she didn't work out.)

Welts relax. Skin rejuvenates and bones mend. It was her words that contained such longevity. That's where the damage settled, festered, and consumed.

"They are coming for you in two hours because you're such an evil boy," she told me more than once.

They were the unnamed strangers, her make-believe agents of judgment, who were going to take me away from my family forever to some sinister location due to my unforgivable little-boy transgressions like being too loud or having an opinion that differed from hers. She would say these words while staring down at me with large, furious eyes and lips that would suddenly turn up at the ends and smile. My mental anguish gave her an unnatural high. Then the countdown began in earnest. She savored these words:

"They're coming for you in an hour and a half. . . ."

"They're coming for you in an hour. . . ."

"They're coming for you in half an hour. . . ."

"They'll be here any minute to take you away because you're such an *evil* boy." . . .

I was left alone with maternal madness. Dad was a house painter who often worked seven days a week for weeks on end. He provided well but was frequently unresponsive. My parents were first-generation immigrants to America, so there was no extended family for me to run to. No neighbor showed a rescuing power. They were what neighbors should be: nice. . . .

Mother relished my struggles and mocked my tears, saying they were illegitimate and groundless—another message that there's something intrinsically wrong with me.

She ridiculed me when I tried to escape her dark proclamations. How dare I exert my will, disagree, use my skills, retain my dignity and value? I would later receive similar criticism from portions of the church.

Wiping away the venom of her words by telling her I wasn't evil only made life harder. Her fury spiked to new and more vicious levels. I couldn't win. I was called every vile, demeaning name in the book, including some foreign ones that I had to look up later in life. It didn't matter, because such spoken assaults, such lethal prophecies, render the same judgment: *You are a void stripped of identity.*

That boys are often emotionally fragile and afraid of the world is one reason they participate more in the martial arts. . . . *Boys wonder if they have what it takes to make it.* According to my mother, I didn't have to wonder: I was worthless. I'd never amount to anything. So give up now.

This wasn't discipline, but destruction. I learned to say nothing, to show no emotion, so she couldn't shred more parts of me. I learned to die among the living.

You're wrong, Mom! I inwardly rampaged. But I made my face deceive and say, *It's okay. This doesn't hurt me.* I remember thinking I'd be better off if I did live with mysterious strangers, and I felt the hole this sickening realization carved inside me; foreign, an unjust invasion against God's good plans for me. It's a desperate thought for a young boy to recognize against his nature that strangers might treat him better than his own mother. It would be much later when I could echo the words of courageous martyr (and Christian *Good* Guy) Stephen: *I forgive you. You didn't know what you were doing.*

I eventually found out that my mom's father was tough on her as a girl. Abuse (like high cholesterol) tends to run in families, holding generations in bondage. Family histories aren't much different than national ones: when you're ignorant of them, you're bound to repeat the same mistakes. . . .

Back to my boyhood. Life lost more and more mystery; again, childlike wonder is a luxury when survival's on the line. I learned to become no one, nowhere. My God-given healthy spirit limped along in hiding. I entered the wacky world of passivity, a haunted house I'd never intended to roam. Worse, fight as I did, some venom made its way into me, ensuring that my journey out of the submissive Christian Nice Guy world would be even more arduous.

And isn't that the goal of our soul's enemy? To get us to think either too much (arrogance) or too little (self-hatred) about ourselves? That we aren't made in God's majestic image and so we don't matter? I have seen evil and I know its ploy: to steal your personhood, your singular God-given identity. Evil tries to completely disintegrate your comprehension of yourself—to rob you of your existence.

I know that if you had markedly different experiences, it's difficult to empathize with some of what I'm writing. Sometimes it helps to remember how you felt when you went without sleep for a length of time. Remember how hard it was to control your mind? How wild your thoughts could become? How you murmured and complained about things that you normally wouldn't have mentioned?

Vince Lombardi said, "Fatigue makes cowards of us all." You go into hiding. People who have been tortured with sleep deprivation speak of how they lost a sense of who they were, and about the resultant hopelessness. They say it was like someone else took over their mind. Now imagine that "no one, nowhere" feeling for more than a night or two—for weeks, month, years.

Why Nice Guys Are "Nice Guys"

Abuse rewires a kid's mind, much as a hacker attacks good software code and rewrites it. The kid thinks he's defective, inferior to his fellow kid, and this is where a lot of Christians, especially preachers, make big mistakes. They say, "Hey, what's wrong with feeling guilt and conviction because of sin?" The answer is, nothing—sorrow and repentance for wrongs committed is right. Sorrow is not destructive; it's a response to what the person has done, and something can be done about it. We can acknowledge our wrongdoing, change our behavior, and experience forgiveness.

But this isn't what Nice Guys specifically need to overcome. *Nice Guys believe that something is deeply wrong with them, not because they are sinners but because they are defective. They become ashamed of themselves as humans, not because they sin but because they exist.* Guilt says, "I did wrong things and am responsible"; shame says, "I am worthless through and through." The latter is anti-biblical, a lie that robs people of intrinsic value.

A sense of who you are gets lost when you undergo intense and sustained abuse or neglect, especially as a kid. You have no real compass to find your way back to who you really are and to fight the lies that assault you. Everyone else, it seems—everyone but you—has the power and the right to mold you, so you drop the sword of your will.

Abused kids harbor a pervasive sense that they are an inferior subspecies, children of a lesser God. When you believe you are inferior to others, you invite fear into the deepest parts of your heart. Men usually don't even know that they've done this, but somewhere along the way, they did, and they've been committed to fear ever since.

Writes Dr. Laura: "It is terrible to have been hurt, tortured, molested, abandoned, ignored . . . or exposed to other demoralizing or dehumanizing behaviors. For anyone to minimize that truth is somewhere between ignorant and insensitive." And when a young boy undergoes such treatment, it creates a "sick parallel universe . . . for you, one that does not allow you to prosper emotionally and interpersonally in your real world with everyone else. Your options and possibilities will appear severely constricted, and understandably, you flounder."[13]

Christian Nice Guys with this background are still sinners. They're not some special case where their sin doesn't smell bad because they had a tough childhood. But it should be clear by now why CNGs drag more baggage through life. As the social philosopher and psychoanalyst Erich Fromm once observed, "The scars left from the child's defeat in the fight against irrational authority are to be found at the bottom of every neurosis."

Being convinced of his worthlessness condemns a Nice Guy to

believing that his life won't and shouldn't amount to much, that he isn't wonderfully made (Psalm 139:14), and that he isn't God's beloved creation, having been crowned with glory and honor (8:5). In fact, living as if he's special to God feels wrong, sinful. He mistakes his self-deprecating beliefs about himself for God's thoughts toward him and his standing in God's eyes; his consciousness and his conscience have been distorted. Grace is an alien concept, because he thinks that God doesn't stop at hating his sin—God hates him as well. Correspondingly, he loathes himself, judges himself by harsh and unbiblical standards, literally bears false witness against himself.

> **WE'VE HEARD COUNTLESS TIMES HOW DANGEROUS AND SINFUL IT IS TO BE FILLED WITH PRIDE. BUT WE RARELY (IF EVER) HEAR ABOUT THE SIN OF THINKING TOO LITTLE OF ONESELF; PRIDE IS THE SAME SIN EITHER WAY.**

Christians are accustomed to hearing about how they should be humble and not think more of themselves than they ought (James 4:10; 1 Peter 3:8). We've heard countless times how dangerous and sinful it is to be filled with pride. But we rarely (if ever) hear about the sin of thinking too little of oneself; pride is the same sin either way. In the former case, it takes the shapes of haughtiness or arrogance. In the latter, the person pridefully maintains that his view of himself carries more weight than what God says is true about him.

Depression and Anxiety

Depression and anxiety also hinder and exhaust passive Nice Guys.

The brains of insecurely attached children react to provocative events with an exaggerated outpouring of stress hormones and neurotransmitters. The reactivity persists into adulthood.[14]

A minor stressor can sweep such a person toward passivity-producing anxiety. A larger or longer one can plunge him into depression's black hole.

Epidemic depression and anxiety cost us more than $50 billion per year, and the massive dollar amounts barely begin to reveal the anguish and pain they represent.

> The mountain is growing: the rate of depression in the United States has been rising steadily since 1960. Suicide rates for young people have more than tripled over that time; killing oneself is now a leading cause of death in adolescence. Reports on child welfare detail their nutritional status, their lead exposure, the design of the straps in their car seats, but omit mention of the stability and quality of love in their lives. We would be wise to pay as much attention to those relationships as we do to the vegetable content of school lunches. . . . In a culture gone shallow, plastic surgery supplants health; photogenicity trumps leadership; glibness overpowers integrity; sound bites replace discourse; and changing what is fades before the busy label swapping of political correctness.[15]

The point? Our society values efficiency and economics over truthfulness and connectedness—it isn't much of an ally when it comes to authenticity and intimacy. To achieve and attain what the culture considers important, men consistently shut down their emotions, disconnect their hearts, and step into the rat race. As a man's buried feelings and unmet needs begin to build up, they scream for his attention and consideration; he has to invest more and more of his resources just in keeping them contained and controlled. Anxiety often grows in him correspondingly, and eventually, if his hidden issues reach critical mass, or if he hits a point of overload, he can spiral into depression and despair, worn down, worn out, and woeful. (More on depression in chapter 4.)

Abandonment and Overprotection

Abandonment, when parents cease to support and care for a child, deals a young boy's heart one of the deepest wounds imaginable and prods him to believe he is unworthy to receive love and affection. Nice Guys spend much of their life salving this wound, often through the consumption of women, both emotionally and sexually. But since they don't yet possess what women really want—for instance, stable support, masculine protection, and real emotional passion—they are destined to lose at love and intimacy if they do not change.

Uniquely, another source of passivity comes from parents who love yet fail to give their kids appropriate boundaries and responsibilities; they take away or shield from life's usual hardships, trying to preserve safety but instead raising passive and timid children. Hara Estroff Marano, who wrote "Nation of Wimps" for *Psychology Today,* says parents are going to "ludicrous lengths to take the lumps and bumps out of life for their children."[16] It shouldn't take secular warnings to awaken the church to realize it's raising a nice generation, a herd of passive kids who aren't being tooled with what they will need for living as adults.

Many think this idea is nearly sacrilegious, but as I (Paul) say on my talk show, kids sometimes need to experience the usual hardships of life. It's the only way they will find out that life's inevitable pain isn't going to kill them, that it can make them stronger. And it will, if we adults help them handle it properly.

> With few challenges of their own, kids are unable to forge their creative adaptations to the normal vicissitudes of life. That not only makes them risk-averse, it makes them psychologically fragile, riddled with anxiety. In the process they're robbed of identity, meaning and a sense of accomplishment, to say nothing of a shot at real

happiness. Forget, too, about perseverance, not simply a moral virtue but a necessary life skill. These turn out to be the spreading psychic fault lines of twenty-first-century youth. Whether we want to or not, we're on our way to creating a nation of wimps.[17]

The young people becoming nice and passive before our eyes are the ones too responsive to the pack's mindset, too eager to fit in, less assertive in the classroom, unwilling to disagree with their peers, afraid to question authority. *All this is the antithesis of real life in Christ.* Talk about a spirit of antichrist.

The sons and daughters of Christian Nice Guys have seen plenty of examples of what it means to live gentle virtues, but do they know *anything* about the rugged ones? We have them isolated, immobile, and reactive (rather than proactive). We're more concerned about providing coddled safety than inspiration. We're raising spiritual veal.

"Your job as a parent is to ease that transition between the idyllic world of the sandbox and the cold world of adulthood as much as humanly possible," says Rabbi Shmuley Boteach. This transition is not achieved through seclusion and isolation, and the failure to implement it is part of how Nice Guys originate.

Fatalism and Detachment

The passive man assumes that others (including you) possess more power than he does or ever will. He's prone to depend on you and others to regulate and arrange his world for him. As you've probably observed and experienced, this makes him undependable and irresponsible. He believes that, regardless of what he does, outside forces determine his future; this is fatalism. He has disregarded the biblical wisdom that if a man plans, organizes, and takes action, he improves the quality of his life. He feels inadequate to handle his life; he's convinced he has little or no influence in achieving what he wants and needs, so even though he's dependent on others, he's resentful of them as well.

When faced with life's challenges, conflicts, prospects, and uncertainties, CNGs go into a holding pattern. They wait, hoping someone else deals with the issues and solves the problems. They hold out for a rescue boat with your name on the side. Many don't expect help from God—they think he's out to get them, seeing as how, from their perspective, they have no worth. Because deep down they're convinced that they're hideous to God, they are not living for him but are instead constantly trying to appease him, even though they think he is unappeasable and unloving, perhaps like their parents.

Other Christian Nice Guys go to the other extreme and believe "All I need to do is give it to the Lord." This common and fatal assumption ignores the truth that we co-labor with God in our spiritual and emotional growth, which are greatly connected. This false assumption is also a hiding place for many CNGs who don't think they can do the soul work required to face their fears and the misconceptions they produce.

The Nice Guy is smiling, but he feels hopeless and pessimistic, which in his mind justifies his reluctance to ask others for help. If things are hopeless, why fight life? Just ease into the arms of fate. If something is beyond his control, that's the way it was meant to be. He may well believe he is working against God's will when he exerts his own; I (Paul) know a man who actually believed his suicide attempt was predestined by God to bring him glory.

Are you seeing why your husband won't share the reins of your marriage? He wants you to take responsibility for your relationship, though he won't come out and say it. But when you do direct your marriage—*someone* has to lead, right?—he may well feel controlled and dominated. He resents you, and consequently you resent him for resenting you.

Nice Guys terrorize their own lives, and perhaps the worst damage comes from their inability to love well, to live out the greatest commandment. Jesus also says to love others as you love yourself, but CNGs unintentionally and often unknowingly produce a pretty shoddy love; when a man despises himself, loving others as he loves himself doesn't add up to much love. *Love and fear cannot coexist. Where one exists, the other is banished.*

Passivity's Life Motto

When life handed them much difficulty, in many cases at such a young age, Nice Guys responded by forming a life philosophy that is unfortunately and catastrophically naïve: *If I live small, my troubles will be few.* This fearful protectionism haunts men and causes them to play everything safe, which kills intimacy as well as spiritual growth, relational potential, and ability to be a protector and provider.

Counselor and bestselling author Kevin Leman says that a passive man is like a "dog when you go to pet it and it falls down on the ground. Why? Because the dog has been used and abused in the past. Same for a passive man. He's got low self-worth. He doesn't think he counts in life. He needs to change how he views himself."[18]

The Nice Guy answers *no* to Albert Einstein's fundamental question "Is the world a friendly place?" His answer, though, is accompanied by his conclusion that life is a realm best rejected and avoided, even as he continues to invest energy into keeping up the appearance of being connected and invested and involved. Regardless of whether he underwent abuse, abandonment, neglect, shame, hyper-concern, overprotection, or anything similar, a CNG believes, *This world has nothing but danger; God must be against me; the key is to keep my head down and avoid attention and conflict.* (Conflict is the CNG's kryptonite.)

LOVE AND FEAR CANNOT COEXIST. WHERE ONE EXISTS, THE OTHER IS BANISHED.

A Nice Guy is emotionally constipated; feelings just don't come out of him in a natural way. I compare my former CNG emotional state to that of my first vehicle, a Chevy LUV. (LUV stands for Light Utility Vehicle. My friends called it Little Ugly Vehicle.) It overheated a lot, not only on hills and in the heat but even on cold days, just rolling around town. It sputtered. It was out of tune. And, like most Nice Guys, it was unreliable.

As a CNG, I wasn't as demonstrative as I wanted to be, but I was at a real loss to know why. I observed other men who went through similar experiences and saw that they weren't as onerous for them. They were more emotionally honest. They didn't feel the same need to hide and to please. Their emotions gave them power and color. I wanted this and was willing to undergo the struggle and the soul work to get it. But even when I extended huge amounts of will, including fervent and honest prayer, no fundamental change took place. Fear and lies had to be confronted and resolved. Prayer alone wouldn't get the job done.

I was concerned that my heart would never engage, that I wouldn't learn how to share and express my feelings. I also worried that I was putting a heartless void in my kids. It was time for change. I had reached a cusp moment where I realized that not acting would be sin. I sought wisdom higher than my own. I saw a counselor, which went against much of the advice I received from church leaders. I am so glad I didn't listen to them and that Sandy supported my life-changing decision.

Force #3: Mellow Messiah, an Insidious Distortion

Christian men across denominational divides are told to follow an example of being and behaving that doesn't exist. They are told to be "like Jesus," but they are shown an incomplete portrait of him as "gentle Jesus, meek and mild." They carry what I call the NGB, the Nice Guy Bible (Retail price: your soul), in which they're encouraged only to underline and study the "pleasant passages" while largely or completely ignoring the ones that can bring freedom from passivity.[19]

This Nice Nazarene is fictitious. The Gospels show a Jesus who was both tender *and* tough, depending on the circumstances. Jesus traveled the entire emotional spectrum without apology. Men who follow a false Jesus hamstring themselves, the constraints nowhere more painful to experience or to witness than in marriage.

> Why is it when someone says, "Picture the archetypal male," the image that comes to mind is not one of Jesus? I have to confess that, for years, the picture in my mind would not have been Jesus. Even the single most famous portrait of Jesus makes Him look more like a pouting model for Breck shampoo than a man.[20]

Frederica Mathewes-Green says, about a mall display of the manger scene,

> [It was] plump with stupidity. Jesus as a cookie. God as a pet. This is very bad news. For one thing, a circle of cuddly bears is useless at helping us deal with pain. It cannot help us grasp searing heartbreak. . . . We want a just-my-size God, fluffy and approachable, without all those picky commandments. But once we get him down to teddy-bear size we find that he is powerless. He is not able to ease our suffering or comprehend our dark confusions; he does not have strength equal to our grief. A reduced God is no God at all.[21]

Philip Yancey once believed in a reduced God. The real Jesus, he writes, is far less tame than the one he found in Bible college.

> In my prior image, I realized, Jesus' personality matched that of a *Star Trek* Vulcan: he remained calm, cool, and collected as he strode like a robot among excitable human beings on spaceship earth. That is not what I [later] found portrayed in the Gospels. . . .

Indeed, he seemed more emotional and spontaneous than the average person, not less. More passionate, not less.[22]

The belief that Jesus was pleasantly innocuous is so ingrained in our popular imagination that I created what I call "The Parable of Jim," taking some of Jesus' rugged words and behavior and putting them into the life of someone by another name. This is a message Christian Nice Guys say has helped them change into Christian Good Guys. Here is a portion:

Jim's a thirty-something teacher to whom people are drawn. But Jim breaks all kinds of rules. He's confrontational, opinionated, filled with willpower.

He threatens to fight scoundrels who are making money off of religion, even grabbing their TV camera, a tool for this sordid gain, and smashing it to the ground, creating one long commercial break.

He has called his students dumb and dull, asking how much longer he'll have to endure their company.

In order to stem his influence, his enemies play word games and devise interview scenarios in which to embarrass him; he's so cunning and shrewd that he constantly shows them up instead. No one has had the guts to talk the way he does. Others talk like they understand God; Jim talks like he knows God. Jim forcefully disrupts the order of things and disregards convention. Jim's inappropriate.

He calls people bad names that "respectable men" never say. He verbally confronts one of his most powerful government officials. When Jim has faced an authority figure who, because of manufactured charges, could actually invoke the death penalty, Jim's slow-to-come responses have been obscure, searing, and disrespectful.

Jim doesn't mind his manners around important persons. Jim causes problems for society's "respectable people." No wonder they want to pull him down. . . .

He has told reporters that his mission isn't to discover or promote a lifetime of warm and cozy. *Au contraire:* "I bring division and conflict! Live as I say you should," he tells morning news shows over coffee and crumpets, and it may "tear your families apart!" Then he states the obvious: "Those who don't find me offensive will be blessed." *Who booked this guy?* Regis wonders, glancing at security, hoping they're keeping a sharp eye. *Who in the world does he think he is?* muse countless others. . . .

Jim allowed a prostitute—in public—to anoint him with rare and expensive oil that could have been used to feed the poor, support missionaries, or pay for part of a child's life-saving surgery. While his students *and* his opponents boiled with anger over this wasteful extravagance, Jim would not hear it denounced and had the audacity to say that whenever God's liberating message is preached, this one event will be mentioned favorably. . . .

Jim is sarcastic, sometimes bitingly so; he doesn't apologize. Jim goes to parties and hangs out with others who do. At least once he has supplied the wine, for free, during a wedding where children were likely present. Drinks are on him, even though he knows he'll be accused of corrupting others and touting sinfulness. The bureaucrats and government works with whom he spends time are the ones everybody else hates. Jim doesn't even shun mentally imbalanced devotees or politically leprous scandals.

Many complain that they don't understand him. His own students sometimes won't ask him questions because they fear his response.

Most religious leaders enjoy the attention of large crowds, but Jim's wary: He doesn't trust them, and he doesn't hide his distrust. He confronts empty compliments during public gatherings—not a seeker-friendly ministry approach.

Jim's been unemployed for at least three years and doesn't even look for a job. He lives off handouts, owns no property, doesn't even have his own cardboard box to return to at night.

Does this portrayal of Jesus look foreign? If we compare these select actions of Christ to the behavior expected of the Christian man in most churches today, and if we're honest, we'd have to say that Jesus wasn't a "Christian." We wouldn't pray to him, we'd issue prayer requests *for* him.

Something doesn't add up, and that something is the Man Box into which men in general and Christian men in particular are expected to fit. By contrast, men who attain marital intimacy do express painful emotions (anger, anguish, disappointment, frustration). Truly successful people endeavor to live wholly, fully, the way Jesus did, and they do not apologize for having normal wants and needs.

Passive Christian men must discard the belief that Jesus was perpetually mild and easygoing. Passive people don't call others a "brood of vipers fit for hell" and "white-washed tombs" (Matt. 3:7; 23:33). Nice Guys don't turn to their followers in seeming exasperation and say, "How much longer must I endure your company?" (17:17). Jesus was not endlessly long-suffering (imagine the false agendas that would enslave him if he were), and he doesn't expect his followers to be either, as seen in the parable of the fig tree (Luke 13:6–9); it's proper to wait for an unfruitful person or organization to produce, but there's a limit to wise patience. Sometimes patience ceases to be a virtue and becomes a naïve vice, and Christian men learn this when they see the real Jesus.

Jesus told us to be wise as serpents. Some versions say *cunning* and others *shrewd*. This makes us cringe. *Criminals,* not *Christians,* are cunning and shrewd—*we're* supposed to be nice, right? No, our mild smiles and mellow moods are evidence that we resist and fear listening to and following Jesus. We largely ignore his parable of the shrewd manager (Luke 16) where Jesus encourages shrewd behavior in those who follow him. Some men's ministries have made nice disciples. Jesus, as found in his own words, wants shrewd ones.

If we do begrudgingly acknowledge that Jesus spoke directly and acted assertively, we tend to say this was reserved only for corrupt and misguided leaders. The truth? It is recorded, for example, that his own disciples "didn't understand what he meant and were afraid to ask him about it" (Mark 9:31). Nice people don't generate fear, they generate head-scratching frustration. This insipid savior we've created, a sentimental cultural icon, wouldn't make those close to him wonder if he'd lost his mind and desire to seize him (3:21).

Characterless people don't use sarcasm, but Christ did, and I thank God for it—I was awakened and vitalized by what I call Christ's "blessed sarcasm." Jesus loves us enough to bother and shock us. If we deny who Jesus was and how he lived, we spin off into heretical belief and doomed-to-fail practice.

Jesus' love for us is too often described in sentimental terms, which is dangerous since sentimental love is incapable of saving a desperate world. Jesus' tough and more penetrating love sets us free—but we have to see it and then believe it. His toughness is a blessing to us, preparing and inspiring us to live well in the real rough-and-tumble world. Tough people expose the lies of the world. Soft people believe these lies and remain shackled.

Biblical Good Guys

Jesus' mama did not raise a sweet little boy. The record documenting Christ's rugged side is there, and it's been there for almost two thousand years. Sadly, it has faded into the background, becoming a lost testament of sorts; the real Jesus is taking a backseat to the contemporary cultural climate, what intellectuals call *zeitgeist* ("spirit of the times/age"). Like car keys on the kitchen table, the true Jesus is hidden in plain view. So is the freedom of millions of Christian men, as well as those who date and marry them.

Contrary to what CNGs think, confrontation can be a path to edification. The author of Hebrews underscores this: "Let us consider one another in order to stir up to love and good works" (10:24 NKJV). The King James uses the uncomfortable word "provoke." Proverbs states that "true love cares enough to confront" and that "better is open rebuke than hidden love" (27:5).

When the apostle Paul confronted and corrected Peter for his inconsistent and cowardly behavior toward Gentile Christians in Antioch, he was engaging in this kind of edification. Previously Peter had practiced open fellowship with Gentile believers; then, when ultraconservative believers came to Antioch from Jerusalem, he separated himself from the Gentiles in order to maintain an appearance of false orthodoxy or purity. In response to this unwarranted and breaking of fellowship, Paul, his comrade, says, "I opposed him to his face, because he was clearly in the wrong" (Galatians 2:11). Peter needed to be confronted, and Paul's correction actually built him up in the faith.

The apostle's letter to Philemon is crafty, clearly not the creation of a Nice Guy. Fighting for the compassionate treatment of Onesimus, Philemon's runaway slave, Paul cashes in some personal chips, holding Philemon hostage to his past good behavior toward him: "You owe me your very self" (v. 20). Paul sets Philemon on the meat hook; he wants him to think, *Paul was good to me—I owe him. He's compelling me to be good to Onesimus on his behalf.*

This is a shrewd move, characteristic of a good soul. A CNG would never have done this—he would have prayed for poor Onesimus, slapped him on the back, and given him a supportive smile, but he wouldn't have the guts to call in the favor. Nice Guys don't impose, even when it's for someone else's good and when justice is on the line. Safety is their God. Their idol.

Pleasant people don't say, "If anyone is teaching otherwise, and will not give his mind to wholesome precepts ... [and] to good religious teaching, I call him a pompous ignoramus" (1 Timothy 6:3–4 NEB). Or, "Why don't these agitators, obsessive as they are about circumcision, go all the way and castrate themselves!" (Galatians 5:12 THE MESSAGE).

These are Paul's powerful words to Timothy and to the Galatian churches. But instead of pondering his words, learning why he used them, and incorporating boldness into our lives, we merely insist that Paul wouldn't use harsh terms or coarse language.

Stephen's passionate defense of the Good News (Acts 7, especially vv. 51–53) is another excellent example of Good versus Nice. Stephen, "*full of the Holy Spirit,*" (v. 55) becomes combative and tongue-lashes his audience, who then stone him to death. Do we get it? He was filled with the Spirit! The Spirit brought him away from correctness and pleasantry, into standoff confrontation.

The people Stephen criticized "were furious and gnashed their teeth at him" (v. 54)—that's enough for us nice-loving Christians to conclude that the Spirit *wasn't* with him. However, our preferences and our avoidance do not make something true or right. *Power* is a word often used in conjunction with the Spirit, and power is found not in insipid passivity and malleability, but in vitality, passion, emotivity, will, strength, activity, and impetus. Do you see? These are among the virtuous attributes men are not encouraged to exercise.

Permeating the Old Testament is the presentation of God as warrior, fighting on behalf of Israel and battling against rebellious Israel.

> It's the Jewish nature . . . to struggle and fight: the name *Israel* means "He who wrestles with G-d." We do not blithely accept injustice, plagues, or hardship. . . . It's not over until it's over, and until it's over, it's our job to fight back with every fiber in our being.[23]

Eugene Peterson, whose *The Message* renders the entire Bible in contemporary language, says he uses the psalms as a means to help perplexed people approach a holy God. They don't think they're good enough to pray to him; Peterson tells them that praying the psalms will "dispel the wrong ideas and introduce you to the real thing." The main wrong idea is the belief that the psalms are the prayers of "nice people."[24]

"Did you think the psalmists' language would be polished and polite?" he asks. The psalms in Hebrew, he says, "are earthy and rough. They are not genteel. They are not the prayers of nice people, couched in cultural language." They contain "immense range" and "terrific energies of prayer," two out-of-bounds elements in Niceland, which firmly restricts movement and resists power. If you won't accept low-voltage living, you'll be voted out. We say, *The sooner the better*.

About 70 percent of the psalms, Peterson concludes, are complaints and lamentations to God. You don't see these verses framed in Christian bookstores accompanied by paintings with idyllic landscapes or a glowing Jesus who just finished getting his weekly facial.

God unleashed a torrent of rhetorical and sometimes sarcastic questions upon Job. Ask yourself: Are the following statements pleasant and nice?

- "Why do you talk without knowing what you're talking about?" (38:2).
- "Where were you when I created the earth? Tell me, since you know so much!" (38:4).
- "Do you know the first thing about death? . . . Speak up if you have even the beginning of an answer" (38:17).
- "Do you presume to tell me what I'm doing wrong?" (40:8).
- "Do you know where Light comes from and where Darkness lives. . . . Why of *course* you know that" (38:19).

You can see where Jesus got his sarcasm. From his Father, who doesn't mince words.

Job was honest with God because he loved God. Their relationship was passionate and personal, even when Job was wrong and didn't have all the answers. Nice Guys aren't honest with God—they hide from him behind a fronted veneer of pleasantry, running from his rich presence. Niceness tries to cover a lack of intimacy with God, and CNGs feel hopelessly stuck because they don't know they're not being—not living—the way they were intended to be.

God is not nice, which means he's not easily offended. He isn't touchy, and he doesn't make us walk on eggshells. He's direct with what he wants from us, and because he is good, and unchanging, he is solid and firm so we don't have to guess what he thinks—the exact opposite of how Nice Guys live.

Christian Men: Dehumanized and Denatured

My friend Michael Levine, who's not a Christian, says he can spot Christians at Hollywood parties: "They worship at the altar of other people's approval." Michael's fascinated as to why Christians think Jesus was wimpy, when even he can read that Jesus wasn't: "Jesus is portrayed as some weak guy who patted kids on the head all the time, and Christian men are expected to follow this example."

Michael, who does public relations for stars, loves Christians. His best friend is a Christian, so he's no bigot. I sometimes want to disagree with Michael's statements, but more often than not I have to agree: frequently, we're the bland leading the bland. We lack backbone. Following a half-Jesus makes us half-alive, dull, unable to connect, missing intimacy.

Rick Warren's *Purpose-Driven Life* could have a sticker on the cover: *The purpose-driven life is impossible to attain if fear is in the driver's seat of your life; you must decide whether you will serve pleasantries or purpose.*

Books about marriage and intimacy should have a similar sticker with these words from a single Christian woman, illustrating just how dire the matter of the passive Christian man has become. "My single Christian girl friends and I have a saying: 'The ideal man to date has only been in the church for two years. That way he still has some masculinity left.'" This woman, who works for a Christian publisher, went on to say that there's *something* about Christian men that makes them less attractive than non-Christian men. They often lack personality, adventurousness, individuality, vitality. And most of them are groomed to be this way!

> **JESUS WAS MEEK TO HIS FATHER'S WILL— NOT TO THE WILL OF MAN.**

Many Christians have a strong it's-wrong-to-stand-up-for-yourself mindset that keeps them from being assertive *and* attractive. One of the main reasons we hear is that Jesus described himself as "meek." No argument, this is true (see Matthew 11:29). But here's the fundamental question: What was he meek toward? *He was meek to his Father's will—not to the will of man.* The Gospels are replete with examples. Meekness—yielding, being submissive, deferring, bowing to—is only a virtue when properly applied. When misdirected and misapplied, it becomes a destructive vice and a hideout for passivity.

Another example is the parable of the mustard seed. Today's Christian has been taught to glean from this story that just a little bit of faith can grow into something so much larger than expected. This is certainly true, but it may well have more meaning, meaning more unpleasant to our present-day ears.

Jesus' parables often were told directly to peasants in small towns, many of whom made their living off the land. A mustard plant growing in their field was not a pleasing sight. A mustard plant is pernicious, invasive, unwelcome; a farmer moves quickly to eradicate it. Jesus may well have been telling his listeners that God's kingdom is an invasive and unwelcomed movement against the powers of this world. We fail to recognize and live out this truth when we pretend that the kingdom goes forth without will, risk, and action.

Recently, on TBN, a female host told a stage full of family men, sitting next to their wives, that one reason men don't communicate as effectively as women is that they "are a little brain dead." Clearly she has an inaccurate grasp of how testosterone, specifically, influences brain activity. However, if a male host said women's brains don't function right, you can bet you'd have heard a protest and perhaps an apology. Dehumanizing prejudice against men is so pervasive that her cutting remark was accompanied not by correction but by laughter.

On Father's Day, at your church, are husbands and fathers honored and encouraged, or is the theme more about their male quirkiness and their goofy habits? Are they celebrated? Praised? Told that they matter, that they're irreplaceable?

After reading Paul's article on Crosswalk.com entitled "Pastors, Don't Use Mother's Day to Bash Dads," a reader wrote, "Your article was so wonderful and encouraging to us fathers. We no longer go to church on Mother's Day or Father's Day because of what is said about men." But it was mostly women who thanked him. "Thank you for your timely article. I couldn't agree more. It's about time someone gave Christian men the support they need."

Numerous men have told Paul that they no longer want to go to church on Mother's Day because they're herded into one all-inclusive category—deadbeat, or thereabouts—and told how insufficient and inadequate they are. One recalls, "Our pastor makes all the husbands get down on one knee and beg their wives to forgive them for being such bad husbands and fathers."

Men have been shamed in church for years with the unbiblical idea that women are more moral and spiritual, that men are intrinsically less so, simply by being male. They have also been given the ridiculous message that if there is anything wrong with their marriage, it's up to the man to fix it, and if the problem persists, it's his fault because he has been unable and/or unwilling to be the spiritual leader of his home. One popular Christian counselor claims that in more than thirty years of counseling, he has never seen a marriage problem where the husband didn't bear most if not all of the responsibility!

Talk-show host and columnist Glenn Sacks says that churches and parachurch organizations unfairly blame men. Sacks, not a Christian, says,

> A Christian advice show on one of the stations owned by my former network here in Los Angeles is a good example—whatever the problem or situation, the two Christian male hosts always fall all over each other to assure the woman caller and the audience that the guy is wrong. The evil Christian patriarchs of the feminists' imaginations sound more like Women's Studies professors—in fact, they're often worse.[25]

What has happened to men in general and to Christian men in particular for generations hasn't been a feminization: *Men have been dehumanized and denatured.* Note, though, that being told to become bland and innocuous is not the same as being told to take on feminine characteristics. This anti-male message isn't making us like women but something other than truly human as made in God's image. We women too have been encouraged, sometimes with good but misguided intentions, to strip ourselves of a compelling personality and true womanhood. In whatever direction, it is *not* of God that any person should undergo destructive transformation. God made us male and female; fully embracing and living out our masculinity and femininity glorifies him in us and through us.

Dehumanization estranges us from our individuality, uniqueness, creativity, passion, and personality. Our lives become routine and mechanical, which tears at the fabric and saps the lifeblood of marriage. We lose vital sensitivity, inwardly and outwardly. We are less able to enhance each other's lives because we have stripped ourselves of the ability to share and receive a truly redemptive power. All this is opposed to creating the intimacy we really want. Intimacy is a mourned casualty of our not being who we are meant to be.

Three powerful forces (a culture at odds with masculinity, the psychology of passivity, and a twisted caricature of Jesus) encourage many men to remain or become passive, to lay down the sword of their will, and thereby relinquish the provision for and protection of those within their care. You've seen how those powers make it hard, and in extreme cases impossible, for your CNG to create intimacy.

But now the good news. These forces pale when compared to the power a good woman has in the life of an average man. No other person possesses your potential to help him move in a better direction. When you use this strength rightly and justly, you can create an environment like no other.

CHAPTER 3

ROADBLOCKS ALONG THE FOUR PATHS TO INTIMACY

Genuine love consistently requires some very hard decisions.

M. SCOTT PECK

You've seen that there are significant, large-scale factors hindering the ignition of desire for intimacy in your checked-out Nice Guy. Please don't let this discourage you, and don't give up before trying, because the good news is that none of these factors can't be overcome. We're living proof!

At the same time, the hurdles *will* require better and wiser ways of relating to your CNG. Furthermore, fundamental differences between men and women make achieving intimacy a challenge in itself. However, with increased challenge comes greater character and greater reward.

When we respect and accept our differences as men and women, it gives love better soil to grow in. Respecting his guy-nature gives a man the freedom he needs to be less strained, more natural, and eventually more intimate with you.

As you go through this chapter and learn about *talking, thinking, touching, and togetherness*—the four paths toward intimacy—realize there's no shame in admitting that your understanding of true intimacy may have been incomplete. That the culture and sometimes the church don't train us well in the ways of love isn't an excuse for being ignorant, but it's a viable reason for not knowing.

It's likely that what you have been doing to create intimacy has failed. It's a good day when you face this and admit it. That means you'll be better able to undertake the challenge of discarding your unworkable script, obtaining the tools for a better one, and learning how to live it. Chances are, your CNG feels pressured, put upon, and misunderstood by you. And, chances are, there are legitimate reasons he feels this way. Comprehending the common roadblocks to intimacy can show you how to pave the road to freedom and closeness.

One Can Ignite It in Two

Before we get into intimacy's foundational basics, know this: there is no law that says intimacy has to be mutual at first. Sure, two people embarking upon the same quest for intimacy is easier, but it's not always necessary. Consider what you see in couples who don't initially go to church. One of them is drawn to a closer relationship with God and starts going on Sunday morning. In time, the reluctant one also begins to attend, not from compulsion but out of interest, curiosity, or desire. That is the difference between *control* and *influence*. The first person doesn't require the other to fall in line; it's the growth and the change that sparks attraction. You, Mrs. CNG, can have this kind of influence.

The path to igniting intimacy in both of you starts with your becoming an agent of change. But this does not include the implicit goal of changing your passive CNG, which is most likely to make him resentful and you frustrated. *Your goal is to change your understanding and your approach.* In so doing, in mustering your own power and ability, something larger and better has a much improved opportunity to form between the two of you.

You, the gardener of intimacy, can't make the plant of intimacy grow. But you can help create an environment that makes healthy growth possible and probable. And, as any honest gardener will tell you, the process will involve a combination of success and setbacks.

Intimacy Defined (It Isn't Love)

Love can live without intimacy, but that love won't grow and deepen without the strength and glue that come from intimacy. We see this in people who have start-and-stop or repeated love interests. Their relationships start off fast, fueled by a natural inertia, Romance Stage 1. But as that fuel source consumes itself, gradually and eventually the relationship behaves like a sputtering, empty-tanked rocket. Momentum and inertia bring it to where it can no longer stay on course or move forward. Not having reached the cosmic space of intimacy, it tilts, one side to another, before it succumbs to gravity and begins its plunge back to earth.

Be around love long enough and you'll know this very well: You can love someone without liking him. There's something about him that holds you, possesses you; your heart is drawn to him, and while other parts of you are repelled, love has a way of short-circuiting your resistance. No wonder we sometimes refer to being "in love" as being under a spell. Loving someone without really knowing him doesn't incorporate and engage all of who you are.

Intimacy brings in your *knowing* him—from his greatest strengths to his most feared weaknesses. It's also having your good, bad, and ugly being known by him—and him doing far more than merely tolerating you. It's the two of you loving and embracing each other, in an all-encompassing way, not only in spite of your weaknesses but because of them too.

Intimacy is the action fuel that turns new love into deep love. It provides a level of closeness that love's infatuations alone can't deliver. Unlike some forms of love, intimacy is not an involuntary result of fleeting feelings or circumstantial emotions. Because intimacy is the work of both time and will, it is far more compelling and more meaningful than a fling of any intensity or variety. This is why W. H. Auden wrote, "Any marriage, happy or unhappy, is infinitely more interesting than any romance."[1]

With romance alone, people enter in, and they exit out. With marriage there is no easy or ready-made exit door from the arena into which two people voluntarily pledge, through remarkable promises, to join and devote their lives. Here, two foreign souls interact, interrelate, and are expected to work things out through the turbulent waters of conflict and resolution, elements of intimacy that create unmatched closeness between two people. Sometimes this room is a love lair. Sometimes it feels like a cage fight. Romantic connections live off body heat, then die. They don't have what it takes to change a person to the core for the better.

We often misconceive of intimacy by thinking of it as a single, isolated act, like a memorable conversation in a romantic restaurant or a pleasurable sexual experience in an attractive hotel room. But those are just stages on which intimacy might unfold. Intimacy isn't an event—it's what happens during these events—two people actively pursuing the other person's deepest being. It is speaking the language of the other person's soul. For example, many married couples have honeymoons, but not all honeymoons are intimate and soulful.

Intimacy includes and involves all our capacities. In the end, the ultimacy of intimacy is two souls risking vulnerability and weaving a life together that couldn't be made without the congealing of wills. It mandates both humility and creativity. Becoming and staying engaged requires that you step outside of yourself and consider him just as supremely important and valuable as you are. Even if his passivity drives you to chocolate.

And it doesn't just happen. Intimacy's fruit is produced when intimacy is cultivated. If we don't connect and share who we are with another, it's a counterfeit. And, as many married couples who have obtained it will tell you, intimacy is deeper, more profound, and more life-changing than they could have imagined when they earnestly said "I do."

Intimacy is not for the proud and the timid; the reward goes to the humble and the brave. For CNG marriages, it's about being honest with how you feel and being receptive to the feelings of others. It's embracing some discomfort and moving forward with love and grace anyway. It's about doing the right thing when the wrong thing takes so much less work.

THE ULTIMACY OF INTIMACY IS TWO SOULS RISKING VULNERABILITY AND WEAVING A LIFE TOGETHER THAT COULDN'T BE MADE WITHOUT THE CONGEALING OF WILLS.

Intimacy is a virtual declaration of war against how we're expected to be and to live, which is give to get. Intimacy gives without the assurance of getting in return. But that doesn't mean it's a foolish or self-abusive giving. Remember: Intimacy is about loving your spouse as you love yourself. The more you love the way Jesus loves—which includes yourself, your spouse, and God—the better example you'll be of living out the greatest commandment.

As with love, with humor, and with grace, there's something innately mysterious about intimacy. You can only explain it so far, and you certainly can't explain it in a single sentence. Eventually you abandon yourself to it and let it take you; this requires risk, faith, courage, humility, and an abiding respect for truth. If you like to hide, if appearing truthful is more important than being truthful, or if you hold on to life too tightly, with too much control, intimacy will pass you by.

Nevertheless, intimacy is not pure mystery either. We help it form and disintegrate, and we have many opportunities to create it. That's the great thing about the future, generally *and* specifically: It comes one day at a time. When we commit to and work at intimacy, we get better at it with time as well.

Intimacy Requires Conflict

Many people attend church to avoid conflict, to escape life's difficulties. Many believe that being a follower of Jesus means forsaking conflict. And now here we go, making the claim that intimacy *demands* it.

The underlying fact, from a Christian perspective, is that marriage is a sacred institution created by God, whose primary concern is not our comfort but our Christlikeness. His will is to increase our growth and maturity, not just make us happy or put us at ease. Life in Christ creates joy that's deeper, stronger, and more redemptive. This joy, like the peace it's intended to accompany, is usually born from and reared through varying levels of discomfort.

Some personal mental conflict is required if God is going to smoke out and show us the lies we carry in our minds. One of the best means for this "uncovering" is intimate marriage. We cannot walk in truth while believing falsehoods.

Our minds are saturated with untrue thoughts about:

- *Ourselves.* We tend to think too much or, like CNGs, too little of ourselves.

- ○ *Others.* That others are likewise made in God's image necessitates a level of respect, even for those who have wounded us or those we dislike. We must push past our prejudices—especially toward passive spouses who do not naturally garner respect.
- ○ *Earth.* The truth is, earth is not heaven, and it's not a gentle or utopian world. Evil has not yet been banished, and it wants to destroy us. For now, we do live in enemy-occupied territory, sharing the domain of devils and deceit.
- ○ *God.* God is neither a bemused, skyward grandpa who cares only that we have a good time nor a rigid, sinister taskmaster who wants to see us suffer. God is the jealous lover of our souls who pursues us with powerful love and amazing grace. He wants us to understand this world's nature for our own good, the way a good parent prepares children for real life. He wants to give us the skills necessary to do more than just survive—he wants us to thrive.

Our misconceptions must be confronted and righted for us to stay sane, live lovingly, and be close with God. Likewise, misconceptions in marriage don't go away on their own. The learning process requires conflict that includes both truth and grace, the way God deals with us. As intimacy guru Paul Coleman says, "Honesty without kindness is like surgery without anesthesia."[2] Those who experience the goodwill and warm regard of redeeming conflict discover that it's a pathway to another world, a bright ray of hope.

This is conflict that's redemptive in purpose and nature. It asks without accusing, observes without attacking, corrects without condemning. Many have never seen this conflict-style in action, and it takes time to learn; don't fall into the trap of thinking you always (and immediately) must do it perfectly. Honest attempts at intimacy create mistakes, missteps, and misunderstandings. Intimacy cannot be birthed or grow without grace.

Many men are flying blind when it comes to this kind of soul-closeness. Writes John Gray, "They rarely saw their fathers succeed in fulfilling their mothers."[3] By contrast, he writes, "A young boy who is fortunate enough to see his father succeed in fulfilling his mother enters relationships as an adult with a *rare* (emphasis added) confidence that he can succeed in fulfilling his partner. He is not terrified of commitment because he knows he can deliver. He also knows that when he doesn't deliver he is still adequate and still delivers love and appreciation for doing his best. He does not condemn himself, because he knows he is not perfect and that he is always doing his best, and his best is good enough. He is able to apologize for his mistakes because he expects forgiveness, love, and appreciation for doing his best."[4]

Intimacy is built upon both positive and negative emotions. Choose to be open to honest statements from him, even if they hurt at first. Limiting your life together to just positive expressions of emotions isn't really living and it isn't really intimate either. Remember: You want to know him for who he really and fully is, and vice versa.

> A marriage is only as good as a couple's ability to fight. A husband and wife who fail to fight are not alive or honest. . . . To claim there was never a failure to love—of omission and commission—is tantamount to saying they've never sinned. Such a lie is blasphemous.[5]

GUY TO GUY

If you're a guy reading this book, on your own or along with your wife, first, let me congratulate you. You've got guts, *señor.* I want to encourage you to keep going, and I want to give you an important piece of advice as well.

Some guys think walking away from a conversation without saying why will make their wives respect them more. This is untrue. If you do this, instead of receiving respect you will receive her fury and feed her beliefs that you are timid, irresponsible, and uncaring. Additionally, this will only make your next interaction with her that much more difficult.

Don't walk away. Consider focusing on the following thoughts that have helped me (Paul):

- I'm not going to hide.
- I will remain present.
- I may learn something important—I'll listen carefully.
- I'll choose to relax and stay focused on the issue at hand.
- I'll strive to get to the real issue.
- I'm uncomfortable, and that's okay.
- It's not wrong to ask her to say something again.
- Something good can come out of this on the other end.

By being present and being real, you'll be able to sift through what you think is true and not true. You won't feel so compelled to collapse and admit to things you didn't do in attempting to maintain a false peace. You can restore and uphold your integrity. You can stop feeling gross inside and resentful toward your wife.

Share with her how it will help you when she speaks without making you feel attacked. Explain how this better approach assists you in not shutting down and in hearing what she's really trying to say. Both of you must stick to the issue rather than making it personal, using God to beat each other into shape, or trying to "win."

About 70 percent of all divorces occur because the couple drifted apart—they lacked the glue of intimacy. Most do not divorce out of such problems as abuse or addiction. Couples lose goodwill, become increasingly detached, and draw up assumptions (frequently false) about the other's motives.

Intimacy demands intention, attention, and action.

Intimacy: Four Paths

Of the four paths to intimacy—*talking, thinking (jointly), touching, and togetherness*—two are particularly attractive to most guys, touch and (believe it or not) togetherness—that is, the way he defines togetherness, which revolves primarily around shared activities, many of which are physical in nature. The other two, talking and thinking together, represent a more substantial challenge *and* even greater opportunity. (We'll talk more about all four of these in chapter 5.)

On average, women derive more satisfaction than men from intimate conversations, whether or not passivity is a large factor. Even if you didn't marry a guy who struggles with passivity, being intimate through talking is usually going to be easier for you than for him.

Here's a general marriage principle: The stronger one in any given area should take into consideration the weaknesses of the other. This is a practical way in which our differences can grow us and strengthen us collectively and build intimacy between us. Regarding conversation, you desire intimacy; a good path to building it, if you are more skilled in this sphere, is taking into account his disadvantages.

Most men are reluctant to reveal themselves in the very sphere where most women are most comfortable with self-revelation. This can create a tendency for you to rush him along or convey expectations that feel heavy to him. Pushing and pressure both squelch the growth of intimacy, which cannot be coerced.

We had a similar scenario with singing in public. Sandy, who grew up in a musical home, sings well and plays the piano and flute; I can play the stereo, but I can't sing. For years Sandy wanted me to share her desire to sing in small-group gatherings, so she put on some not-so-subtle pressure. This just made me more reluctant and increasingly frustrated.

I finally explained that asking me to sing in public is like my asking people to take out a notepad and write a quick story, then collecting the sheets and reading them out loud. For most non-writers, this would be a mortifying experience. What's a person to do if he's expected to be what he isn't?

When your man does reveal himself through words, really and truly listen, seeking to hear him without judging him. And be realistic. Don't mandate marathon conversations. Intimacy will likely be short at first. You can begin to turn small talk into intimate talk if he feels listened to, respected, cared about, and understood. Most important, he *needs* to trust you with his real, genuine feelings. The importance of this need cannot be overstated.

Trust and "Fixing"

The word *trust* is related to the Middle English word *troth,* which means "truth," "loyalty," "faithfulness," "a person's pledged word."

> To trust another person is to count them as a person who loves the truth. It is not merely a matter of being honest; it is being a person who loves integrity and can admit when truth is lacking in their life.[6]

Christian writer and counselor Dan Allender was dismayed to find out why, after nineteen years of marriage, his wife told him a painful story from childhood that she'd never before shared. She said, "I trust you now in a way I didn't a year ago." When he asked what brought this about, she answered, "I don't know, but I do know you are more open to hurt for me rather than try to fix me."[7] This is a man who counsels people regarding trust.

Wives also tend to desire to fix their husbands. Some theologians teach that this desire wasn't originally there, that it's a result of the Fall. In Genesis 3:16, God, speaking of sin's consequences, says that wives will "desire" or have a "longing" for their husbands, and the word "for" may imply an antagonism. This pivotal text could be rendered, "Your desire shall be against your husband, and he shall rule over you."

Tuned-in couples know there is an inherent power struggle in the marriage relationship. Men often have extreme reactions to power: either passivity or domination. Women often have a desire to gain and maintain control. However, sin's corruption of the intended marital harmony is where God's grace can shine through. He tells us we can restore it through mutual submission and a willing acceptance of love's truth (Ephesians 5:21–33).

The desire to control and to "fix" men is dangerous, and it extends deep into Christian circles. "Fixing" men frequently means taming them, and a tame man usually isn't a good man—he's likely dropped his sword, surrendered his will, and turned from his own nature and identity. Odd how our noted strengths can become our greatest weaknesses! In this case, a woman's ability to love her CNG with words can so quickly turn into a shaming assault.

By contrast, a healthy conversation between husband and wife is open, curious, and sometimes playful. It's neither a must-win debate nor a statistical droning on of information-providing. "In some ways," says Allender, an intimate conversation "is like brainstorming."[8] Emotions must be present for intimate conversation; you can help him keep his emotions present by treating him well as you communicate.

The Cancer of Contempt

The great killer of trust and emotional revelation is contempt, the belief that the other person is worthless and deserves scorn. Studies at the University of Washington's "love lab" have found that contempt is the best predictor of whether a marriage will make it. The greater contempt's presence, the higher divorce's probability.[9]

Contempt attacks, blames, and dismissals are all part of what turns men into CNGs in the first place. Contempt is an effort to make you big and someone else small. It will appear in your tone, eyes, words, body language—contempt can be conveyed in myriad ways, and whenever it shows up, it cripples intimacy. Contempt is so lethal that it can be harmful to proceed with attempts at intimacy before the issue is faced. Contempt must be named and transformed before even conversation has any hope of intimacy.

Furthermore, contempt is the *modus operandi* of evil; the name *Satan* means "accuser." Accusations are generally not invitations or explorations; they are intended to humiliate, disempower, and make others vulnerable to manipulation. Contempt's goal is to discredit and steal dignity so the victor can remain in control, unfazed by any differing view or idea.[10]

Another gender difference is that men usually don't demand as much from relationships as women. Writes Paul Coleman:

> Men are more tolerant of other men's ways. Their friends can be loud, obnoxious, rude or self-centered and the guys still might get a kick out of being in each other's company. That sense of lightness, of not needing or expecting a great deal from a friendship, can carry over to a romantic relationship. The average guy, to his mind anyway, overlooks a lot of annoying things about his partner. "My needs are simple," a man might say. So when his partner has higher expectations of him, he can get resentful. "I'm so accepting of her, why can't she be more accepting of me?" he wonders. Women usually want more depth to their relationships. Men get comfortable with the status quo.[11]

In learning to connect with your guy, make sure it doesn't seem like a demand. It should feel to him like an open door to enrich your lives together.

Male Dependency

Here's something you can't afford not to know: Men are conditioned from birth to seek the approval of women. Most guys are raised by women, and most go through elementary school with far more female than male teachers. Many have grown up in homes without fathers or with limited exposure to them. By the time you get him, your guy has received countless messages, spoken and unspoken, on what women expect from him; his male nature likely has been mishandled by some important woman or women in his life, and there was probably someone who didn't allow him to be guy-like or encourage him to embrace and live out his masculinity. Chances are, he's well-trained in saying and doing what women want, but not in sharing what he really thinks, needs, and wants.

A guy often has built-in barriers to being straightaway honest around women. He thinks that if he speaks his mind like he does around guys, he'll just get himself in trouble ... and in a way, he's probably right! Even passive men tend to be more straightforward with other guys. Many men can rumble through a war of words and be friends soon afterward. Conversely, you may know from experience with other women that female exchanges of harsh words can carry forward emotionally for years and even fatally wound a relationship.

When a man gets into an argument with another man, he pretty much knows what he's in for: It's one on one. When he argues with you, it can feel like he's battling several of you. You're probably better with words, and he can feel like he's defending his island against a small army. (Or, if you're really hitting hard, like he's up against Medusa, that Greek mythological creature with serpents for hair.) Experience has taught him that the battle with a woman isn't over when the words end; an underground (and unfair) campaign against him can go on for weeks, months, even years if he doesn't toe the line. For some husbands, passive or not, being honest just ain't worth it.

For most of his life, your man has likely been dependent upon women for a good portion of his happiness and success, and that makes it difficult for him to stand up to you and stay engaged with you. Though he

HE NO DOUBT FEELS THAT IF HE IS COMPLETELY HIMSELF WITH YOU, YOU WILL REJECT HIM.

probably doesn't articulate it, he no doubt feels that if he is completely himself with you, you will reject him. If you want him to be forthright and connected, you need to prove to him that it's okay for him to speak what's really on his mind—otherwise intimacy won't happen. More so, when he does make mistakes, that your love will not be withdrawn from him. He needs to feel comfortable knowing that he does not have to have all the "right" answers—that is, the "right" that is defined by most women.

One dramatic example of this reluctance, broadly, is found in blended families where the husband finds it nearly impossible to stand up to his ex-wife, especially with custody issues. When he won't stand up to her, his new wife feels unprotected, unloved, and reproached. *Who's he* really *married to?!* worms through her mind. Dr. Laura says, "Men will do what women tolerate." He feels trapped between pleasing his new wife and living by a lifelong script of trying to please all of the other women in his life. It's a no-win situation.

When a passive man does muster the immense courage to stand up to an ex-wife, usually after years of pleading, it's a painful process to watch—it can be like a volcano letting loose. He has never been naturally assertive with women; now, pressured into response, he blasts forth in often overblown ways. A man who rarely raises his voice—maybe hasn't done so in years or decades—can explode when he feels completely cornered.

Pause to Consider

One final matter: you probably need to evaluate what's going through your head about your CNG. Chances are some of your thoughts are inaccurate. For instance, maybe you have said to yourself or to a friend, "It doesn't make sense why he behaves the way he does." Not true. It makes a ton of sense. There are reasons he has learned to live small and behave passively; fear and hiding are not the right responses to struggle or trauma, but they are not inexplicable or pointless, and thinking or suggesting that they are can lead you into contempt and indifference.

If you still feel there is no explanation for why he doesn't yet give and receive deep love, and why he doesn't foster and uphold intimacy, we recommend that you reread chapter 2 and then read chapter 4, keeping in mind his actions and words and habits as you read.

He doesn't know what intimacy really is; you must be willing to help him learn. If you have been using an intense and critical demeanor, you will need to alter it into a listening and constructive approach. You'll know that what you are doing is working because you'll sense him leaning into you (not away from you) emotionally.

Though the misconceptions and related obstacles on the paths toward intimacy are real, and though some are more substantial than others, they are not set in stone. A wise woman of goodwill, who uses her innate influence to love and to heal in facilitating emotional closeness, is a source of magnificent power.

CHAPTER 4

EMOTIONS OF THE CHRISTIAN NICE GUY

How can you say, "I love you," when you won't confide in me?

DELILAH, TO A CONFUSED SAMSON (JUDGES 16:15)

K nowing more about what intimacy is and isn't, let's turn our attention to the specific reasons Christian Nice Guys struggle with intimacy in marriage.

As we saw in chapter 2, the goal of CNGs—*living small*—is no way to live. This approach leaves him muted, undercut, and diminished. Additionally, the life-script from which he takes his cues makes him emotionally unavailable, leaving you out in the cold.

Here's one of many letters that I (Paul) have received from men struggling with CNG-ness:

I'm a recovering Christian nice guy. Being "nice" and friendly was a personality that I hid behind for years to protect myself from my fears. My Christian parents unintentionally taught me to be afraid of making people angry. So I became the nicest guy as a way to hide from life and other people. It has been damaging to my friendships, and when I backslide into the Christian nice guy lifestyle, it really harms my marriage!

It harms his marriage because the passive heart is troubled, fearful, and conflicted. He's fighting so many internal battles that when it comes to life with you, he seems to be going through the motions of marriage, consistently shut down and difficult to reach. As you'll see, he doesn't realize that his *heart* is required to create intimacy with you, with others, and with God. He thinks following all the rules will sustain his relationships. He doesn't yet know that intimacy comes not from checking off a to-do list.

You don't need us to tell you how his silent retreat from much of life makes you feel abandoned, resentful, and unprotected. Your emotions are valid and self-evident. But you likely do need additional insight into the reasons he hasn't engaged. Once again, life factors have profoundly affected and impacted his heart; remember that passive hearts are made, not born.

This chapter is like an MRI into his emotional state. It will help you get to the elusive *why* of the matter. It will help you see that for the most part the problem is not about you—at least at its core—and you'll be better able to offer empathy, seeing why a different approach can move your marriage in a better direction. As Sandy experienced, seeing where he's coming from helps you to stop taking his lack of emotional availability so personally.

Fear: His Retreat

Put yourself in his sweaty running shoes, an appropriate metaphor because he's always running from something. Christian Nice Guys are motivated and controlled by fear.

If you haven't seen the movie *Ella Enchanted,* please check it out. Even though there's nothing cute or romantic about what he does, the CNG is like Ella. Played by Anne Hathaway, Ella is a young woman under a spell where she has to do whatever others demand of her. Her will is superseded. Her life becomes a mess. Like your CNG, she unintentionally hurts others. She's consumed with internal conflict and self-loathing. Her personal boundaries are nonexistent (she doesn't know where she ends and others begin), and she has the disease to please.

"Under a spell" is a helpful way to view where your man is: entranced by fear and its henchmen. How did it happen? As we've seen, passivity often develops during childhood; many Christian men got it from their religious experiences; all men are prodded toward it by a culture that denigrates them and doesn't value the strength and wisdom of their insights and emotions.

A few years ago, a bestselling book called *The Gift of Fear* was released. While its author made some good points about the nature of fear, it would have been better if he'd used some different terms. For instance, instead of telling us how good *fear* is, he could have shared with us the benefits of *caution.* The fact is, from a psychological perspective, fear isn't a gift to a lot of people. It freezes them into sitting ducks and makes them suckers for manipulative lies and agendas. As we see from Ella, the figurative spell of fear destroys personal boundaries, and intimacy is among its most tragic casualties.

> We must accept that fear is not only harmful but evil, not only unhelpful but deeply destructive.[1]

A great way to make FEAR an acronym: False Evidence that Appears Real. If two people, one who doesn't struggle with fear and one who does, experience the same uncomfortable event, they will respond very differently. The passive, fearful person will perceive a huge problem (mountain out of a molehill); he's likely to freeze up, but he'll try hard not to show it, covering fear with nuanced deception. (If he's passive-aggressive, he might attack those who point out his deception.) The assertive, non-fearful person will likely see it as cause for concern but will proceed with intelligent carefulness.

FEAR AS AN ACRONYM: FALSE EVIDENCE THAT APPEARS REAL

Most Christians are familiar with the truth that "perfect love drives out fear" (1 John 4:18). What we often don't consider is the inverse: Fear casts out love. Fear behaves like plastic wrap around the heart of a CNG, ensuring that his underdeveloped emotional side will neither receive nor give deep and abiding love. Fear is intimacy's #1 enemy.[2]

Uncomfortable in His Own Skin

An adult who was raised in an abusive, cold, or unstable home tends to approach intimacy in one of two ways. He is likely either to crave intimacy and be over-needy but go about it so wrongly that you might assume he wants something else entirely, or he'll fear intimacy so much that he comes across as distant, indifferent, and closed-up to closeness. Consider this: He may have a hard time trusting you, not because you are untrustworthy, but because you are human. He has a hard time trusting anyone, including himself. He's not at home in his own skin, and deep within he doesn't believe it's a good thing to be human, that who we are, who he is, has worth and value.

One of the most significant outplays of this is his fear of and flight from emotions; to him, they often represent the absolute worst of what it means to be a person, to be alive. Passive people the world over have difficulty expressing emotions, and guys, on average, have a harder time expressing emotions, so it's a dual challenge for a passive Nice Guy to be emotionally available—a prerequisite to being intimate.

Two main reasons: negative emotions (1) make him feel out of control and (2) may well remind him of painful memories. He has yet to reach the other side of the feelings, where tears of sorrow show themselves to be liberating, cleansing, and clarifying. Walking through the emotions, instead of fleeing them, makes a man feel more alive, more prone to pardon and to love.

However, saying this to him is often like telling a depressed person he's depressed and that he needs to try harder so he can change. His state of mind is so prevalent and long standing that it sounds to him like he's being told to believe in an alternate universe. He doesn't yet realize that there's a good side to all emotions, and he's lacking a measure of faith that could help him to see.

Clipping negative emotions and painful experiences also clips positive emotions and pleasurable experiences. An ironic example is the problem of impotency: the inability to sustain an erection or halt premature ejaculation is often related to submerged or unresolved anger and anxiety. A man who in this way distances himself from painful feelings and emotional intimacy simultaneously distances himself from joyous pleasure and physical intimacy. Passive men deny the reality that God created us to feel.

CNGs go to church primarily for comfort and safety (in opposition to God's plan of invasive and stretching redemption). Similarly, he adheres to a belief that marriage should be primarily about comfort and safety. But intimacy *isn't* just comfort and safety—thank God it's so much more than that.

Lovingly discussing, processing, and sharing emotions is invasive, and that's a good thing. God is love, and love is good. The paradox of love is that it provides comfort and discomfort (sometimes together). It feeds hope, gives power to forge ahead, brings clarity and resolve. Love moves stalled lives. Love is a messenger of change; love changes people, and passive people fear change.

People already committed to transparent honesty and vulnerable truthfulness view an emotionless guy with bewilderment, suspicion, and even disdain. He seems other-than-human because his humanness is stilted, so how to connect with him? Other than in sporting venues or in physical activity, where is he likely to feel deeply? Where is he invited to be himself? (An ideal venue is in your home. We'll get deeper into this later in the book.)

Christian men need to be encouraged and shown how to harness their emotional power to help create emotional bonds. Our goal needs to be becoming like the real Jesus, who was *not* a Steady Freddy or a flat-lined stoic. In some church circles, emotionally vacant men are mistaken for spiritually stable and mature giants. The pressure to conform to this false ideal can be overwhelming, and many (or most) don't have the strength to resist it.

The Defensive Man Only Defends Himself

While working on this chapter, I (Paul) went to a nearby coffee-house, where, at separate times, I observed two couples in conversation, each couple with one other person. In both cases, the interaction was sometimes heated (one involving homeschooling), and the husbands literally said almost nothing. The wives handled the entire debate; neither was defended or supported. The husbands allowed another opinionated guy to hold court over an entire conversation, even when their wives were rudely interrupted mid-thought. One husband hid behind a laptop, the other kept leaving to get more food.

The wives did all the talking not because they were bossy but because they knew they would need to do it alone. They were accustomed to their husbands not engaging in conversation; the guys are fearful that they've got something to lose if they speak up, so they remain almost silent, perpetually distract themselves, keep their hands in their pockets, maintain pleasant expressions, and count the seconds till they can leave.

An aggressive man, explicitly or implicitly, may even make a move on a passive man's wife in the man's company. He can, and he knows he can, because he senses that the passive man, somewhere in life, dropped his sword. The passive man senses something foul, but he buries it—he won't give a public display of affection, a physical move into the offending man's social space, or a direct *I know what's going on* look. These not only make him feel uncomfortable, he may even think they would be sinful actions.

Remember his training: A good Christian turns his cheek to all wrongdoing. However, the meaning of Christ's admonishment is to not return evil to evil; that isn't synonymous with protecting your wife and marriage. He needs to step up, his wife wants him to step up, but the odds are against him.

Some well-meaning expressions of what we call Christian living have taken the man out of me, some since Sunday school. Being intimate requires emotional integrity, and that, for the CNG, is counter to experience. He'll have to go against the flow, especially his understanding of "good Christian behavior," to live differently and come alive with you.

One example from our early years relates to music. Sandy grew up thinking that Christians should listen only to "Christian music." I, growing up in a nonreligious home, doubted this; plus, I found that other kinds of music, especially jazz, got my blood going and stimulated my vitality. I used to say, "I don't want to listen to music that preaches at me—if I want a sermon, I'll read my Bible or buy a tape series."

While Sandy didn't initially meet my perspective or my choices with open arms, this is an intimate illustration of how I, who wanted to feel alive, had to go against conventional thinking that I didn't think was entirely biblical. Your CNG probably has similar desires to express himself but comes up against ideas more connected to man-made tradition than scriptural truth.

Depression and Ownership of Life

As we mentioned before, some CNGs also struggle with depression, which further diminishes and marginalizes emotional engagement. Research shows that lack of parental support during childhood is associated with increased levels of depressive symptoms and chronic health conditions (e.g., arthritis, hypertension, urinary issues) in adulthood; this association often grows more prominent throughout adulthood and into early old age. A man in this stage is often anxious and ill. He thinks harshly and poorly of himself, and he believes he is a victim of circumstances.[3]

Symptoms include: loss of interest in activities he once enjoyed; feelings of sadness or emptiness that last more than two weeks; change in appetite (gaining too much weight, or losing too much too quickly); sleep disturbances; general feelings of restlessness, hopelessness, and worthlessness; anxiety, irritability, and fatigue; workaholism; chemical abuse (drugs and alcohol can mask signs of depression and make it harder for others to detect the issues); difficulty making decisions and concentrating; thoughts of death or suicide.

Of particular interest is depression in older men, which can be harder to detect in the presence of health factors like heart disease, stroke, or cancer. These conditions can cause depressive symptoms, and medications for them can also have depressive side effects. However, according to the American Psychological Association, "It is critical to identify depression among the elderly because they, especially older white males, have the highest rates of suicide."

According to the National Institute of Mental Health (NIMH), about six million American men suffer from depression annually. Yet men are far less likely than women to seek help not only for all mental-health problems, but depression in particular.[4]

Depressed men are not only less prone to talk about these feelings, but they often need to be pointed out for him to see and realize what they are. Depression involves the suppression of emotions, and when pressured, over-stimulated, or stretched beyond his resources, a depressed man can snap into outbursts of anger and rage.

His depression includes a spiritual component: he fails to see that God desires ownership of his life, not because God is a grand puppeteer but because man rightly belongs to him, and if man rejects God, something else "owns" him. When God owns a man, he guides that man to live lovingly and responsibly by his grace. Authentic, willful Christian living terrifies the CNG. He doesn't want to be responsible for his life because he believes he's incapable of living it well; he feels that if his life is up to him, then there's no hope. So he wants others to administrate his world and make decisions for him; commonly, his wife is his surrogate.

If we were puppet-like, choice-less beings, the book of Proverbs, for instance, would make little sense. A study in assertive, proactive living, Proverbs tells us that we influence the quality of our lives for ill or for good. Proverbs can serve as a profound antidote to the Christian Nice Guy malaise.

One reason both you and he deal with such confusion is that his lack of ownership for his life is not (or is rarely) obvious to him; if asked, he's not likely to say, "I don't take responsibility for who I am." It isn't laziness that tells him to stay separated from engagement; rather, fatalism tells him he must always submit to the will of others to prove he's a "real" Christian. This brings him to conclude that his life is the result of other forces and wills. If the quality and direction of his life are largely out of his control, his choices seem inconsequential; this flawed thinking about God, himself, and others likely makes him feel insignificant. If he responds by burying his emotions, he is a candidate to become depressed.

People need to have a sense of being before they can have a sense of well-being. More so, CNGs need to know they have a will in order to understand that their choices absolutely do matter. Saying yes or no to others comes from a realization that you are a whole person, that you have valid wishes, dreams, and desires. When you're whole, there's a clear line between where you end and others begin.

Nice people don't have such clear lines or clear thinking. Nice people think others have more worth, so others have the right to dictate and determine. Nice people believe it's ungodly to have boundaries over time and energy. If you changed Jesus' name in the Gospel accounts where he avoids people in order to be by himself, a CNG would call his wise behavior selfish.

PEOPLE NEED TO HAVE A SENSE OF BEING BEFORE THEY CAN HAVE A SENSE OF WELL-BEING.

Being honest about what he thinks, developing the ability and desire to speak his mind, and learning to be straightforward with emotions will make him more real. He will feel like a genuine, legitimate person, and with the acknowledgment and validation of his mind, will, and emotions, he will become more able to say no when it's best. It's a life-changing process and, for the CNG, an open door into a whole new dimension of intimacy with you.

LETTER FROM A READER:

My husband sees himself throughout *No More Christian Nice Guy*. He decided at some point that he must avoid anger and conflict at all costs. He's become the great pretender. It's more important to look good than live good.

Our marriage has never been intimate. I try to draw him closer but he won't come to me. Why don't guys realize that if they would be more vulnerable and honest with us that we would love them more, not less?

Paul's Response: I don't know your husband or the reasons he won't open up. I can only speak from my own experience, which is pretty common for passive guys: I felt that I would be criticized if I were more honest with my feelings. I'm sure my childhood had something to do with my reluctance. Also, Sandy would sometimes try to get me to express myself too quickly. And when I did, she sometimes would be critical. She didn't intend to hurt me, but she did. So my fears were confirmed pretty early in our marriage. I needed to do some soul work, and we needed to approach each other differently.

Sandy's Response: I wanted Paul to open up more and take a stronger stand in life. And when he didn't, I just did what most people do: I put the pressure on. Now I see how I needed to back off, create space, and approach the problem from a better angle.

Uncomfortable With Feelings About God

Jesus said he came to bring us abundant life, but he also told us that this life is difficult to find. Small living is nowhere near abundant living, but instead of choosing humility, instead of acknowledging how weak and unfulfilling his lifestyle really is, the CNG redefines "abundance" with a subjective and contemporary interpretation. Boldness, passion, and purpose are reduced to obedience to the will of others (not God) and to the submersion of his emotions. This is dishonest—often deceptive—and it halts marital intimacy.

There's no shortage of ways for a Christian Nice Guy to twist spiritual insights and then hide behind them. We shouldn't ignore how convenient and safe this deception is. He's got a lot of company behind life's curtain. His own pastor may be back there with him, living off the same misguided script.

Again, recall that he likely feels inside that it's wrong to exert himself, to be fully human, to have desires, needs, and a functioning will. He has probably attended churches, read books, and attended retreats that fortify this belief. He's been told to not "try to make anything happen," that he's supposed to "just pray about everything" and watch God spin into action.

Talk about a theology of passivity. Here, God's sovereignty is taken to mean that the expression of the identity God gave him is neither important nor required. The essence of Christianity, he has likely been told, is (1) avoid sin and (2) evangelize others. He thinks he must get rid of his individuality.

He mistakes difficulties and obstacles for God's sovereign will. If he's been told that it's "worldly" to be shrewd and to plan, he's not likely to push himself to do his best as a provider. He doesn't believe in self-care and self-direction, which makes him docile. He's missing his rudder, so using his motor seems aimless and tiring.

When a CNG reads in his Bible that God is jealous and that God is love, it's largely academic. *That's nice,* he says to himself, and quickly moves on. He'll read the parable of the prodigal son, perhaps Christ's most poignant story, like he's reading a recipe: study the main characters, try to come away with a moral to remember. Without his emotional hang-ups, he'd see and feel God's unbelievable love and forgiveness working its way deeper and deeper into his emotional core. Warmth might spread throughout his body; he might shed tears of joy. This awesome truth of God's nature would spur him to love others in the same way . . . if only he could feel. But he can't feel a deep love for God (or others) the way God (and you) feel about him. Instead, he settles for mere do's and don'ts, and an endless array of check lists, which do not lead toward intimacy with anyone.

Rule-Bound

CNGs read parts of the Bible they can already relate to. All the stuff about God loving them, for example, is pretty much unnecessary fluff, for "weaker people." They largely skip ahead in order to find the *real* stuff: what we're supposed to do. Oh, the blindness of fear and passivity!

The CNG has a backup plan, just in case others don't rescue him from difficulty: Follow The Rules. Even though these rules may not be biblical—in fact they may be man-made—he follows them anyway. For one thing, conflict is always wrong (even though Scripture says it can be a source of edification and strength). For another, the will of others must be carried out, regardless of whether it's right or good, and he calls this "Christianity" (though the Bible tells us otherwise).

Being independent requires conflict and responsibility. The truth is, some CNGs aren't in their marriages to create something good but, rather, to keep from having to be independent.

Some men likewise become Christians not because they are responding to God's love and want to live for him but because they think coming under the umbrella of a framework of rules means they won't have to engage their injured hearts. The problem with being rule-bound is that rules don't spur emotional connection. Freedom does. Again, intimacy is nurtured, not coerced. This is one reason CNG marriages must avoid hyper-spiritualism, rigidity, and legalism. Remember, he doesn't know that your relationship will thrive from the presence and engagement of his heart—he thinks good behavior alone is the answer.

THE PROBLEM WITH BEING RULE-BOUND IS THAT RULES DON'T SPUR EMOTIONAL CONNECTION. FREEDOM DOES.

Your CNG wants to be told what to do because rules are safer than intimacy with God or with you. He prefers the rules because he thinks that once he completes them, he'll have God's approval, and he won't have had to get close to God to earn it. Same with you and marriage: If he keeps the primary statutes (don't get angry with her, don't cheat on her, hold down a job, put in face time with the kids), then he's met his requirements, so *get off my back*. Rules are his protection and defense—his legal counsel, so to speak, for avoiding problems. If an issue arises, he can avoid having to interact with emotions by appealing to a legal code that he can recite, escaping real life by using "the rules" to remain disengaged. Once more: Passivity is tricky.

Vivacious Women, Malleable Men

The state of a passive man's troubled heart frequently becomes more pronounced when he enters marriage, especially given the kind of woman he's likely to wed. For reasons too common to be coincidence, CNGs often marry vivacious women. *Our people* tend to marry *their people*. And, as one recovering CNG jokingly said, there's a fine line between vivacious and vicious.

These marriages are frequently like a dramatic movie plot, sometimes comedy, sometimes tragedy. Screenwriters know they must boost the tension level with escalating conflict, so they meld wildly different personality types, and we get to watch the sparks fly. It's great in film, because films make us laugh and cry. Not so enjoyable in real life.

As the CNG is attracted to vivacious strength and energy, so the woman is usually attracted to calm, unflappable steadiness, thinking this is part of a quiet strength in him rather than a disconnected passivity. Early on in our life together, we exemplified this—I was pleasant, pliable, charming; Sandy was straightforward, assertive, and protective.

Then the tick-tock of the marriage clock showed us another side of our life. It felt like a cruel joke, but in reality it was a path toward greater maturity for both of us. Remarkably, the very qualities that drew us together eventually were pushing us apart.

Another frequent factor to keep in mind in CNG marriages: Just as he tends to sit back or shut down when it comes to spiritual matters in marriage and family, she tends to adhere to extra-biblical preferences and treat them as gospel. This is to say, such wives are hyper-spiritual. Common examples include inflexible church attendance (however many times weekly), even when the children are sick and should be resting instead; narrow interpretation of Scripture, even when another interpretation doesn't conflict with the essentials of orthodox belief; special visions from God; and tendency to put multiple church commitments above normal home-life responsibilities.

Hyper-spiritualism is an intimacy killer. Not only is he reluctant to tell her what he thinks and feels, he also has to go up against an unreasonable and demanding presentation of God. Says Gary Thomas:

> If a woman essentially abandons her family to ambitiously "serve" God, she will likely display the same lack of compassion and empathy for others as she does for her own family who feel her absence keenly. I've seen these personalities. Whether in men or

women, there develops an underlying ruthlessness, a demanding spirit, and a stark self-absorption that permeates every task and relationship as the person seeks to manipulate others into joining their own orbit rather than seeking to launch people into God's. There is a veneer of religiosity, but a polluted, foul smelling spirit reveals itself as soon as you get underneath the surface.[5]

NAGGING

Honesty time. The common response when a CNG wife comes up against her guy's emotional thinness includes unkind words and a sharp tone. Guys have a word for this: Nagging. Repeatedly going after him with increasing frequency and intensity will push him deeper and deeper into his ice cave.

Paul thought I was a nag. Which was partly true and partly unfair. Someone has to step up and give what is essentially a State of Our Union Address, and that sure wasn't going to be Paul, CNG, PhD. So pointing out ominous problems doesn't make you a nag. (It made me heroic.) It's *how* you point out marital trouble that makes all the difference. The key: Avoid the extremes. You need to be something *between* a doormat under his feet and a rolling pin over his head.

Delilah said to Samson, "'How can you say, "I love you," when you won't confide in me? . . .' With such nagging she prodded him day after day until he was tired to death" (Judges 16:15–16). Samson was goaded to reveal the secret of his strength. A CNG is goaded to reveal the bound portions of his heart; words like Delilah's have likely come from your lips or bounced around in your mind.

"Oh, how I have been there," says author and speaker Liz Curtis Higgs, "nagging and prodding until my husband couldn't bear another word. Worn to the nub, just like Samson." So Higgs, warm and wise, came up with a new commandment: "Thou shalt not whine." It's "good advice for those of us with a tendency to snip, snip, snip, at the people we most love. When I'm tempted to complain, I hold my tongue—almost an aerobic activity."[6]

The opposites-attract-until-they-attack scenario stunts intimacy. Both people tend to get rigid quickly. Flexibility and willingness to try new strategies (see chapters 9–10) will help build a bridge back to one another.

A Picture of Hope

We've written a lot about what life looks like with a checked-out CNG, someone who sees only indifference and even hostility toward what he feels, who doesn't grasp the impact or effect of what he does and how he lives. We want to show you a little glimpse of what life looks like when both husband and wife get their intimate groove on.

Sadly, we can think of more couples who don't possess it than do. The ones lacking intimacy always have at least one person reluctant to engage emotionally. The other, frustrated with trying to get him or her to be more real, resorts, eventually, to haranguing. They are angry, and at times it's palpable. The other recoils and often stews in resentment.

Couples that possess intimacy show grace and goodwill. They fight *fairly*. Emotions flare, but they don't belittle each other. They disagree yet leave the other intact, challenged but uncut. They don't withdraw their love and respect.

They aren't high maintenance. Breaking bread with them is enjoyable, humorous, and without a lot of arbitrary rules. Their company can be light and serious during the same course.

And we're glad to see couples who were at war begin their journey toward intimacy. Their coming together is almost always preceded by one's spiritual growth, rarely both at the same time. The change in one stirs the other. "It" appears on their radar, though they may not be able to see what it is. Gradually and increasingly they lean toward one another and engage.

For me (Paul), intimacy was a blessing in disguise. I wanted a more intimate marriage. I could see that I wasn't doing my part to help it grow, but I didn't know why I was so reluctant to reveal myself and get closer to Sandy. I was genuinely bewildered and frustrated; so was she. I was willing to try something different in order to live more, even initially being uncomfortable.

The odd fact was, this at first also felt uncomfortable to Sandy. During date nights, I began to ask penetrating questions designed to help her open up more. While I wish I could say I came up with them on my own, I got them from an outstanding booklet, *Creative Conversation Starters for Couples*. (We highly recommend this resource—well worth its price.)[7] Asking the right questions, then responding in a non-pressured and genuinely interested fashion, is a fantastic way to help your CNG come into the open. There are no wrong answers when he does.

I would memorize two or three questions on the drive home from work, even writing cues on my hand so I'd remember. Now, for a change, I was the one pursuing Sandy! The questions, along with a good meal and a good glass of wine, really threw fuel on the fire of intimacy. Sandy began to look forward to these nights even though some of the questions challenged her.

Sandy was taken out of her comfort zone when I stepped up to life's plate and started saying things that had been on my mind and had kept to myself for years. Much within these conversations related to her legalistic upbringing, a common dynamic in CNG marriages.

"I cried more than once and felt deep anger toward Paul. Why is he doing this to me?" she kept asking herself. "All the while God was changing me as well, and I didn't even know it."

When your CNG rouses from beneath his passive slumber, he will fight back, disagree, challenge, probe, and point out your weaknesses like never before. The great news is that this, too, is also part of what is bringing him into being married *and* engaged.

The common phrase "I'm a lover, not a fighter" shows how far off we are when it comes to creating intimacy. Men of ferocity generally make the best lovers and the most intimate partners. They have obtained the kind of wisdom that helps them disagree fairly.

Intimate relationships are comprised of people who know their identity and worth, and, as a result, take better care of themselves and how they relate to one another. They tend to their relationships. They know they have a large say as to the

> **THE COMMON PHRASE "I'M A LOVER, NOT A FIGHTER" SHOWS HOW FAR OFF WE ARE WHEN IT COMES TO CREATING INTIMACY.**

quality of their lives. They don't control every aspect, but they are better stewards of the parts they manage. This is what people can do when they're not paralyzed with anxiety. Bob Dylan sang many years ago that you're going to serve *somebody;* wives of CNGs know the heartache that comes from this service being given to fear.

Earlier we stated that CNG marriages often follow a dramatic story line in which two very different characters are written into the same scenes in order for sparks to fly. Please consider: That scriptwriter, the one with all the incisive and well-placed lines, may well be God. Consider that he may have put the right person in your path, your marriage scene, so that not only can you be an agent of change in his life but so that he may also serve to bring change in you. You may show him boldness and assertiveness he likely will not have obtained without you, and he may bring compassion and understanding you wouldn't obtain without him. We find great strength when we are willing to engage and share our weaknesses.

CHAPTER 5

GENDER DIFFERENCES AND INTIMACY LANGUAGES

Hell . . . is the suffering of being unable to love.[1]
FYODOR DOSTOYEVSKY

We usually approach life assuming that others see things the way we do. One element we often don't understand is that how we view life is affected by the result of our biological creation as men and women. Our wiring doesn't make us better or worse than the opposite gender; it makes us human and unique. When gender harmony is reached between husband and wife, you see it as part of God's hallowed work and you praise him. When disunity is reached instead, you might see gender harmony as unobtainable and be tempted to curse him instead.

A rigid and undetected gender-locked perspective quickly leads to anxiety, frustration, disappointment, anger, and resentment. These happiness-robbing feelings will be in play until we recognize our differences and then, more importantly and harder yet, learn to accept them. They don't go away.

Skill and wisdom regarding gender differences is key in any marriage. But it's even more essential in CNG marriages because of the specific obstacles to overcome. The greater the challenge, the greater the need for additional insight. And, bluntly, the wiring of most women makes it more difficult for them to relate to and connect with a CNG. We want to show you how to work through the primary areas of problem and struggle.

Throughout most of human history, if you made the assertion that men and women are different, people would wonder what other boring statement you were going to say next. Not because you'd be challenging their thinking, but because they'd assume you were going to make another point. If you didn't, you'd merely have stated the obvious, as if you'd said, "Hey, everyone, two plus two equals four."

The sad fact is that throughout much of history, gender differences have been used to dominate and diminish women; in many ways, for many moons, men behaved badly. During the latter half of the twentieth century, in response, a concerted campaign was waged in an attempt to establish that there actually are no real differences between men and women. Part of this was designed to liberate women from stereotypes and practices that have held them down. This admirable work went overboard, however, when it attempted to deny and "eradicate" all differences between the genders.

One gender is *not* better than the other. We are *equal* even as we are *different*; advantaged in some ways, at a disadvantage in others. And it's not as though we live in different realities. We see the same world. We just, on average, tend to focus on different parts of it. Accepting this helps us to cease trying to make each other more like ourselves; specifically, it helps CNG wives avoid trying to "fix" their men. (This, by the way, is the main complaint men give about women. The number one complaint women have about men: They don't listen.)

Intimacy Through Talking and Thinking Together

Women often go where angels fear to tread. That women are more likely than men to talk about relational matters—regardless of whether there's a Nice Guy factor—sets into motion some profound challenges. Women, in desiring more intimate conversations, are more tolerant of emotional discomfort. Men tend to shut down a conversation quickly if the discussion gets emotionally unpleasant. Though experts debate the reasons, some contend that it may have to do with his ability to get forceful when angry. Stepping back may be his way of avoiding violence, saying or doing something he's sure he will regret.

Relatedly, women are much more likely than men to discuss problem areas more harshly, especially at the beginning of dialogue.[2] CNGs don't do harsh talk—it turns their ears to wood. It also halts *your* ability to turn conflict into an intimate moment. "Verbal assault" is one reason it's easier for a guy to talk with other guys. They are widely more accepting and less judging of one another.

TO REPLACE A HARSH BEGINNING

You need to sell your criticisms or complaints in such a way that they will be heard. Open with a graceful but still-honest conversation starter. Here are some possibilities. (And remember, what you say after initiating conflict should be designed to win the battle for intimacy, not to be right or to defeat him.)

- "I'm angry about something, and I'd like to talk about it."
- "I know we've talked about this before, but I need to bring it up again. I'll try to be brief."
- "You might not like what I'm about to say, but I need you to listen and see if there is anything that has merit."
- "I know that you see things differently than I do about this topic, but I'd like to try finding some common ground."
- "This isn't easy for me. If I twist my words, please give me a chance to get it right."[3]

Don't forget: Wise as a serpent, gentle as a dove.

He's Not Uncaring, He's Unilingual

It's probably not the case that your husband withdraws from arguments out of being indifferent or uncaring. Chances are, he's flooded with emotions that he doesn't like and has allowed to build up. Some emotions he's afraid of, and he feels ashamed of his inability to express them. When he does dare to express them, they may come out fragmented or disorganized, the way someone speaks in a foreign language when not yet fluent. Finding the right words can feel exhausting; he's also trying to gauge whether you're okay, he's digging himself into a hole, or he's about to be attacked. Describing what he feels is sometimes hard.

He will disengage if he feels you are waiting to pounce on his every word. We've heard frustrated wives describe such men as "stupid." Whether or not someone is disadvantaged or underdeveloped, telling him he's dumb is cruel and disrespectful. Doing so will only create or exacerbate an unsafe, disharmonious environment. Ask yourself: What's my goal? If it's to prove that he's wrong, you will probably be trying to prove his guilt and bring him down. If it's to come together, to be understood and known and embraced and loved, bring open heart and open arms. Don't use honey-we-need-to-talk as an outlet to get a pound of flesh.

I (Paul) happen to be comfortable speaking unscripted, on the spot. On my show, I love taking unscreened calls and talking about whatever comes across the lines. My skills in this area give me deep empathy for passive men who struggle to express (or despair of expressing) themselves. But I also tell it straight: the fact is that these men *must* embrace and learn an emotional language. Statistically, they are headed for divorce court, and the primary reason given by the wives (usually with children) is not abuse or infidelity but rather a general feeling of a lack of love, a lack of appreciation.

Part of this is that many men define love differently and live out their love differently—that is, they speak it in another language, one that tends to be more action-oriented and less sentimental. It isn't wrong for a man's love to be shown practically; it's that he needs to develop additional tools (verbal and emotional) to round out and expand his portfolio. Our hope is that you can understand and empathize with this deficiency, then approach it from the angle of seeking to help your man through it, similar to how you might help him through the difficulties of a physical illness.

> **IT ISN'T WRONG FOR A MAN'S LOVE TO BE SHOWN PRACTICALLY; IT'S THAT HE NEEDS TO DEVELOP ADDITIONAL TOOLS (VERBAL AND EMOTIONAL) TO ROUND OUT AND EXPAND HIS PORTFOLIO.**

Included with women's greater verbal skills are more highly nuanced observations; they also use more words. Talking is one of their power centers, just as physical strength is generally a power center for men. Men have rightly been encouraged to restrain and donate their physical power in order to create greater equity and harmony in marriage. Likewise, women can restrain and donate their verbal acumen in order to create a more level playing field. Sandy had to learn to govern her verbal cache, and I had to learn to pump mine up—which was so much easier when I didn't feel under siege.

In this essential area, by and large, wives hold the power in their relationships. They help grow intimacy *when they use their power justly*. Rather than compelling you to strong-arm your husband (as Sandy once did), this special ability can lead you into humility and temperance, the way someone well-trained in martial arts will do most anything *not* to fight, instead seeking to make peace through other means. Embracing personal power is a profound antidote for fear; fear is one of the main reasons fights begin in the first place. Using your power wisely can help countless circular arguments reach resolution.

Adopting a Learner's Stance

For many men, expressing a wide range of emotions is like standing in front of a crowd naked. It's among the bravest things they'll ever do. (We're not recommending that as an undertaking of bravery.) To an average guy, revealing his heart feels something like the equivalent of your moving toward the rat in the kitchen or killing the big spider on the wall with your fingers. So when he does express himself fully or even halfway at first, it's like a small miracle. It's a sacred moment when a timid soul exposes itself to the eyes and potential criticism of another. He needs your understanding, not your critique, during such a moment. You are the strong one in this area of life. Lend him your strength, and give him room to imperfectly express himself.

From my work as a newspaper reporter and editor, one particular insight has been helpful to the wives of passive men. Contrary to what some believe, reporters do not tell others how the world *should be* (that's done by columnists and in the editorials); reporters tell how the world *is*.

When interviewing someone, I don't try to correct. I ask questions and, even more important, I listen. I'm not trying to get a person to "say the right thing." I'm trying to encourage the expression of what they think, feel, believe.

During these conversations, as much as possible, think of yourself as a reporter, with one big qualifier: Listen with care. That is, don't endeavor to be objectively distanced. Smile when you're able; aim for compassion, the way you'd be compassionate with someone else who's been through hardship. Your goal isn't first to impart what you think is "right" but rather, up front, to understand where he's coming from and, possibly, what he might be running from. He needs to trust you with his feelings. Correcting or attacking his feelings diminishes trust.

No amount of quoting the Bible will change this, nor should it. Don't say something like, "You're a Christian. Pray about the problem, then get over it." Prayer is not a way to elude life. Prayer is an action that calls us to commune with God. Prayer doesn't necessarily make pain go away; more frequently it helps us better and wholly walk through the pain life brings.

I (Sandy) used to say things like this. I gave spiritual directives that didn't minister, mandates smothered in condemnation and shame. Married men usually have very few close, trusted friends; you may be the best person in his life to express God's love for him. Don't misspend this unique opportunity to minister to him and create intimacy with him. Become a minister of hope—hope is the antidote to his pessimism. Draw closer to God yourself. Study his Word as it relates to hope, and share your insights with your CNG.

The Two-Edged Sword of Female Feelings

As I (Paul) say on my show, "Women have a leg up on us when it comes to relationships. We need to listen to our wives—they see things we sometimes don't." Specifically, writes Hara Estroff Marano for *Psychology Today*,

> Women's perceptual skills are oriented to quick—call it intuitive—people reading. Females are gifted at detecting the feelings and thoughts of others, inferring intentions, absorbing contextual clues and responding in emotionally appropriate ways. They empathize. Tuned to others, they more readily see alternate sides of an argument. Such empathy fosters communication and primes females for attachment.[4]

Men, on the other hand "focus first on minute detail, and operate most easily with a certain detachment."[5] In other words, they systemize. And their detachment can cause hard feelings and create distance.

We see this difference between the genders online. A broad survey of U.S. Web usage has found that though Internet users share many common interests, men are heavier consumers of news, stocks, and sports while more women look for health and religious guidance. A study by the Pew Internet & American Life Project found that men are slightly more intense users of the Web; they log on more frequently and spend more time online. "Once you get past the commonalities, men tend to be attracted to online activities that are far more action-oriented, while women tend to value things involving relationships or human connections," says Deborah Fallows, a Pew researcher and author of the report.

One factor [to remember] with the phenomenal female ability to bless others with empathy and related forms of connectedness: like all good things, it can go overboard.

Females are set up biologically to internally amplify their negative life experiences [like living with a CNG]. They are prone to it psychologically as well. . . . Women ruminate over upsetting situations, going over and over negative thoughts and feelings, especially if they have to do with relationships. Too often they get caught in downward spirals of hopelessness and despair.

It's entirely possible that women are biologically primed to be highly sensitive to relationships. . . . [But] there's a clear downside. Ruminators are unpleasant to be around, with their oversize need for reassurance.[6]

If you overstate your emotions as they relate to relationships (and if your guy tends to dismiss emotions, a common CNG mistake), and if you want to draw your guy out of his hiding place, you will want to keep a close eye on how much emotion you display. This doesn't mean you don't express yourself. It does mean you'll want to make sure that *how* you express yourself is concise and does not overwhelm him.

Christian or Not, Nice or Not—He's Still a Guy

Many in the church have been led to believe that when a man becomes a Christian, he should become more like, well, a woman. When this doesn't happen, Christian wives can feel personally ripped off.

Many of the problems we faced in our marriage were misdiagnosed. We went to churches that told us our differences were spiritually founded. *Women are more spiritual than men,* they said, so the answer was pretty simple: Paul needed to be more woman-like.

Paul chaffed. Eventually, he dug deep into this prevalent falsehood and presented another view. Now we understand that much of what we once thought was spiritual was gender-based. A peace treaty of sorts followed.

Writes Nancy Kennedy for Focus on the Family,

> D. James Kennedy, Chuck Swindoll, James Dobson, my hus-
> band—they all burp. Guys burp. With gusto and obvious delight.
> My point in all of this is simple: men are not women. . . .
>
> Unfortunately for most husbands, it often takes their wives a
> long time—if ever—to realize that. Too often women blame their
> difficulty in communicating and relating with an unbelieving hus-
> band on their unequal yoke. *If he were a Christian, he wouldn't feel
> the need to take off in his truck and drive around for hours by him-
> self.* But that's not the case.[7]

Guys do like to burp. Though not on the record, Moses probably
burped. So did Peter and David and Abraham.

Anyway, Kennedy creates a crash course in Masculinity 101 by list-
ing the top eight guy behaviors that women ought to know. Three deal
with fear: fear of losing control, fear of being thought inadequate, and
fear of being a hypocrite. One behavior is a subset of these three, and
it's the biggest one wives of passive husbands need to know: Guys are
cave dwellers when problems strike.

It's a male tendency that exists even in non-passive men. They are
prone to go someplace in their minds or someplace spatial, like a garage.
Paul does work around the house and goes for bike rides. He carries a
recorder everywhere because it's during these times, when it doesn't look
like he's solving problems, that he often comes to his best solutions.

The point: The appearance that he's checked out from life, avoiding
everything, doesn't always make it so. How can you tell the difference
between grabbing the remote control out of avoidance or out of the need
to step back and analyze? He will come to you with his response, though
it may not fit your timing and/or be the "right" answer. Allow a reasonable amount of time to pass and set a deadline that's mutually agreeable.
Then let him be.

Remember that for men, doing things alone is very important. It reminds them that they're efficient, powerful, and capable. They rarely talk about their problems, and when they do, they want it to be high-level, expert information—in a sense, they want to have it already worked out. Asking for help is seen as a sign of weakness. This doesn't justify reluctance to ask for help, but it can help you realize that often it makes him feel small, and no one likes feeling small.

Place your nature in perspective: to most women, advice does not signify weakness but strength. You see it as evidence that you care and support him. And it's true. But that's not how he perceives it, especially when in fear's grip; in that state, when he gets advice he didn't ask for, it feels like someone publicly displaying just how incapable he is. Advice, for him, isn't a path toward better living but a device of exposure and call-out. If he feels trapped, he may try just about anything to get out of the spotlight.

Here's a good example. Paul has taught a number of guys how to fly-fish. At first he tells them everything they need to know to make a good cast. This is usually done on a nice green lawn, without a fly on the end. When they have the basics down, Paul takes them to an actual river, puts on a fly, and let's them go. He still gives them instruction, but there comes a point where if the man continues to disregard his help and repeats the same errors, Paul will not help that person further—unless he asks for help. It's because, from a guy's perspective, he doesn't want to embarrass the other man. It's part of the guy code. Messing up a cast is a lot less embarrassing than having a guy continually pester you with advice.

This is a foreign concept to some women, who are used to both immediate and sustained encouragement, support, and direction, which do not feel embarrassing to most. This is one reason why you need to ask your CNG to give you what you want instead of waiting for him to voluntarily give it to you. In many cases, a husband won't automatically help his wife, not because he doesn't care, but because it goes against the male code.

This can go against the notion that if you have to ask for help, the help doesn't really count. But as the above demonstrates, this is not how many men think. (In fact, if a guy offers advice without being asked, other guys call him a "know-it-all" or a "jerk." Such men give other men the creeps. And your man doesn't want to be a jerk to you).

> **YOUR ADVICE IS FAR MORE LIKELY TO BE HEARD AND ACTED UPON WHEN HE PERCEIVES HE'S BEING APPROACHED AS PART OF A PROBLEM'S SOLUTION, NOT THE PROBLEM ITSELF.**

When he *requests* help, however, a man appreciates advice. And your advice is far more likely to be heard and acted upon when he perceives he's being approached as part of a problem's solution, not the problem itself. Motivate him by making him feel needed.

When a man ruminates over problems, such as at work, with money, or in the home, he's likely to become preoccupied with them until a sort of light appears and a solution presents itself. He'll go into solve mode: an intense, analytical, and relatively unemotional phase of thinking. He's prone to figure out the problem on his own, rarely bringing the topic to committee. At least at first—it's how he's wired.

Women, by contrast, are inclined to take an integrative and intuitive approach. This means you're more tooled to ask others for help. When your man goes into solve mode, please don't mistake it for rejection.

Paul goes into "coach mode" around one hour before a game, and he stays in it during the game through about an hour past the game, win or lose. Abby, our only daughter, and I have learned to accept this three-hour window that's devoted to the execution and analysis of soccer. We know it's not a good idea to talk to him during this time, though Abby sometimes sneaks over to the sideline for a hug.

At the same time, Paul does his best to be at least civil, and he gives her a kiss. From his perspective, expecting him to be open to conversation, discussing other topics during this pivotal time, is simply unfair, given his need to focus intensely. He assures me that it physically hurts his head when he's asked to do so. Being true to his nature in this respect is not a sin. It would feel wrong to him if he didn't focus this way; he'd feel he was giving his players and their parents less than his best.

NOTE TO THE NICE GUY

What would really help your wife during problem-solving mode is telling her that you don't know the answer but will get back to her when you do. And then get back to her! Don't use this as an opportunity to coast in your relationship, hoping she'll forget about what needs to be handled. That hasn't worked in the past, and it's also a lie—it hurts her, angers her, and undermines her trust in you.

Remember, she's more likely to verbally address relationship issues than you are. A wise man respects her inclination. No woman wants to be married to man who seems like he doesn't care.

Once again, of the four primary paths toward intimacy,[8] most men prefer two (*touching, togetherness*) and most women prefer two (*thinking, talking*). Just as much emotional gridlock and frustration take place when we try to make our spouse prefer our favored intimacy forms, much personal growth and marital harmony come about when we stop trying to force the other person into our intimacy box.

Some men have flawed thinking about intimate thoughts and talking—they believe it's synonymous with being controlled. Many think that emotional connection will make it easier for someone to "get" them, lock them up, hold them captive. Some have wounds and scars from a female figure who, once he exposed himself emotionally, took advantage of his vulnerability with attacks, criticisms, punishments, or manipulations. Regardless, though—whatever his reasons—he needs to come to see and believe that he loses *nothing* from true intimacy. He will gain vitality, passion, safety, and so much more; he just needs to know and feel that he won't be controlled or taken advantage of.

Intimacy and Togetherness

Generally, women are more skilled at and fond of recalling past events, especially experiences that created a common emotional expression. A man's memory is usually drawn toward shared events and activities. As we've all experienced, intimacy that lasts is often based upon recalling past enjoyment. What a man remembers, what gets his happy juices flowing, are intimate moments with you that center around shared experiences that are active and physical.

This is why a man is glad to see his wife push past her fears and jump on the back of his new motorcycle. Sure, he bought it to enjoy the exhilaration that only bikes can deliver, but what he'd love is to share that action-intimacy with his wife. It hurts him to hear his wife denounce his purchase as selfish, even as he begs her to put on a helmet and leathers and join him.

Dancing is another venue for intimacy that's born from physical and active pursuits. Learning ballroom, tango, and other forms of dance has been among the most enjoyable and intimate experiences we've had as a couple. Not only does it feel good to learn them, it's also good to be humbled together while you struggle to learn. Sharing the same learning experience brings a unique form of intimacy. Mutual "embarrassment" is fun when you don't play the blame game.

Another way we've cultivated active intimacy is through fly-fishing.

It doesn't matter that Paul is better than me—he enjoys showing me the basics with both dry and wet flies, and I enjoy the setting. The first time out I caught seven trout, and he tells me he's never seen anyone look so good in waders.

When a man partakes in an activity with his wife that she engages in with a joyful spirit, his heart leaps toward her. She grows in stature; his emotions soar. *Not only do I have a lover,* he thinks, *I have a friend, a true partner.* When she does it condescendingly or bitterly, he wants to both run away and push her away; she's insulted him and belittled his enjoyment.

You likely prefer intimacy created through deeper thoughts and words—the sharing of the emotional contents of both your hearts. Even though that's difficult for most men and sometimes even overwhelming for a CNG, don't think it's impossible for him to learn to express and share this way. We aren't asking you to compromise what you want. We're encouraging you to obtain a more skilled and realistic way of forming and upholding what you want.

Your preferred forms are important and shouldn't be discarded. We want you to see that if you desire intimacy with him, you will first need to move in his direction; passive people usually don't make the first move toward intimacy, or, for that matter, toward anything meaningful. This isn't because they're bad or stupid. It's because shackled people tend to stay in the same spot.

When you do move his direction, you'll see that your chances of creating intimacy in other areas will expand as well. We suggest sharing some activities he enjoys. Afterward, as you bask in the enjoyment together, ask a question or two that explores feelings. Endeavor to keep it somewhat light, at the start. Seek to build on the good feelings he has. Use your intuition, your innate ability to discern as you learn.

Intimacy and Touch

Sex always brings the possibility of volatility. "No other topic bears more potential for intrigue, humor, hurt, or hope. Like a loaded gun, it is to be engaged with respect and wisdom."[9]

Sex smokes you out because it's the hardest venue in which to hide. Given the requirements of vulnerability and honesty, sex is an altar of amazing reckoning. Just as it's stomach-turning to share a meal with someone you dislike, intercourse without resolution of marital strife can be stomach-turning as well. Physical connection in the face of emotional distance can make you feel that you're desecrating something precious.

For sexual intimacy to flourish, you must come clean with one another. Sexual connection, done well, brings God glory. Other couples see the intimacy you're fostering, notice the rarity of both depth and playfulness, and ask for your secret. With your life you're saying, "The most crucial theological truth about sexuality is that God loves sex and evil hates it."[10]

Says David Schnarch:

> What is most human about human sexuality is our unique capacity for intimacy. It takes guts as well as gusto to get any of the glory. . . . [S]ex that comes naturally is reproductive sex. Intimate sex, however, is a learned ability and an acquired taste.[11]

Sex, he writes, can be more than just a euphemism for making love.

> It can be the actual process of increasing love, of sharing it, of whetting our appetite for it, and of celebrating life on its own terms. This process . . . is actually built into the nature of committed relationships. It happens almost spontaneously; the hard part is going through it. . . . Intimacy . . . is not always soothing and doesn't always "feel good." It is, however, how we forge ourselves into the people we would like to be.[12]

If we *don't* engage the fullness of sexuality and refuse or fail to build on its unparalleled wonder in marriage, we have no idea what we're missing.

> Strange things happen when we have sex at the limits of our potential. That we hear so little about the spiritual side of sex reflects how few people ever reach their sexual potential.
>
> There is time stoppage. It is a consequence of profound involvement.
>
> There's also a lack of awareness of pain. I work with people who have arthritis. I advise them to have sex in the morning, so they will have less pain—but to have less pain they have to be involved.
>
> There is a laser-like focusing of consciousness. There is often a vacation-like sense of transportation.
>
> Age-shifting is another phenomenon. You may be holding your partner's face in your hands and suddenly see, in a very loving way, what he or she will look like older, or exactly what [he] looked like when [he] was eight years old. It is very moving.[13]

If you're married to a CNG, though, chances are you've had to contend with "covert contracts." Rather than being straightforward about his needs and desires, without telling you, without being assertive, he shows affection with the expectation that you'll return his affection and that this will then turn into what he wants. If it doesn't, he either blows up or pouts, and you're confused. When you ask, "What's wrong?" he sins and says "nothing."

He's afraid to be honest with his sexual needs. His upbringing, his history, and/or his learning from the church may have fostered shame in him for having normal longings. While he wants you to regulate and administrate his life, he constantly battles his own God-given nature— he's got desires, but he's thinks there's something wrong with them, and he would need to be assertive to initiate their fulfillment.

His confusion and unpredictability set you on edge. If he refuses to take charge and instead makes you guess, what are you to do—how can you even know when you're supposed to be guessing? Instead of representing intimate joy, sexual connection can feel dangerous and tremulous.

Sex Really Is That Important

Scripture celebrates sex within the context of wedded bliss, but you wouldn't often know it from the way many churches or Christian media presentations address it. The reasons are both varied and comprehensible.

> It should be obvious why the church so often falls on the side of repression, rather than celebration, of sexuality: No human longing is more powerful, more difficult to rein in. Sex has enough combustive force to incinerate conscience, vows, family commitments, religious devotion, and anything else in its path. How the church got its reputation as an enemy of sex is a long story, in some ways shameful and in some ways understandable.[14]

Our culture has lost its mind regarding the value and responsibility of sexual activity. The world promotes pleasure without consequences; the church has countered by understating pleasure.

This does not bode well for CNGs, who consistently tell us that their biggest area of marital discontent is frequency and quality of sex life. While they know something is missing, at first they aren't happy when I (Paul) explain that they bear responsibility for mediocre stabs at emotional closeness. Their ways make them unattractive; their mindset short-circuits their emotional awareness and their sexual connectivity. Sex is not meant to be robotic or sterilized.

Nevertheless, as with many pain points, this area is also a place of fantastic opportunity for you. This realm of discontent can be the very place from which cultivated intimacy spreads and causes further growth and closeness in other parts of your lives.

We've noticed that in our own marriage this is a two-way street. Sandy, like many women of her generation, did not know early on just how important sex is to a husband. We get stacks of letters from Christian husbands about this; they note that their wives don't even perceive sexual intimacy as a key component to a man's happiness and often treat it as a hassle or an extracurricular activity.

Many wives have the right theology, go to the right schools, attend church regularly, and are well-trained to raise healthy children, yet don't see the value of regular sexual intimacy with their husband. Part of this, no doubt, is due to exhaustion, especially for mothers. Sometimes people feel they're simply too busy to cultivate intimacy.

You need to know this: Sex is as fundamental a desire as food for most men. Something dies inside a married man when this desire isn't met. Sex shouldn't be the only reason a man marries, but it's a biggie. As I have said many times, if men, especially younger ones, say they aren't getting married to have sex, they're probably already having it.

My writing on the importance of sex in *No More Christian Nice Guy* got so much positive feedback from CNGs that we want to share some of it with you now. Many said it explains

SEX IS AS FUNDAMENTAL A DESIRE AS FOOD FOR MOST MEN.

exactly how they feel but never could put into words. One said it was so meaningful that he broke a long-standing tradition and underlined long sections. Some who read it out loud said their wives found it to be an eye-opener into the heart of their man.

A Christian man struggles to maintain sexual purity in a culture that says he's crazy. (Once I told co-workers that my wife and I waited till after marriage, they looked at me as if I'd just gotten off the shuttle from Pluto.) In a common scenario, an unmarried Christian man knows he could have sex with many women but he withholds and endeavors to wait. He fights back temptation after temptation to please God and to give his future wife the gift of purity. Then at last he marries and crosses the finish line, yet instead of fabulous banquets, he gets frozen dinners for years. Such men will tell you they feel robbed, resentful, that they're victims of false advertising.

Women, sexual intimacy tells a man that you care about him and him only; it's how he feels special. It is to men what chocolate, diamonds, peaceful homes, and memorable vacations are to you. Sex is our *Lifetime Network,* our *Oprah.* It's the closest we get to being those screaming, insane girls at a Beatles concert. Our days, like yours, are often arduous; sex is where we feel that all of our sacrifice is worth it, appreciated, noticed. Sexual intimacy freely given somehow stabilizes our universe. It's our action to your words, our shelter from the storms of life; you are the safest harbor in which we'll ever make port. Sex is also the sharpest, most jagged knife in our back when it's not given or, worse, given without passion, focus, and interest. We can tell. Our pain is far more nuanced than you realize.

Attempting to ward off or at least cope with the hurt, Christian men try to joke about it. Here are just some of the names I've heard to describe unsatisfying sex: check-her-pulse sex, did-I-detect-life? sex, refund sex, mercy sex, pity sex, I'm-tired-so-hurry-up sex, 50%-off sex, 9-1-1 sex, undertaker sex, wouldn't-pass-lie-detector sex, jewelry sex, new-car sex (but rarely sex in the car), and bigger-home sex. *What we really want is There's-No-One-Like-You sex.* That's our physical and emotional Promised Land, and there are too few of us making camp there. We need your help!

I've heard a Christian man say to his wife, in front of a full dinner table, "I'll get you back someday" for rarely being "in the mood." It wasn't the merlot talking either. It was his spurned heart crying out sideways. Lifeless sex whispers or shouts the same horrible message to all of us: *insulting*.

Here's a somewhat famous letter, circulated among disgruntled husbands, that tries to assuage their pain with humor:

To My Loving Wife:

During the past year I have tried to make love to you 365 times. I have succeeded only thirty-six times; this is an average of once every ten days. The following is a list of the reasons why I did not succeed more often: it was too late, too early, too hot, or too cold. It would awaken the children, the company in the next room, or the neighbors whose windows were open. You were too full; or you had a headache, a backache, a toothache, or the giggles. You pretended to be asleep or were not in the mood. You had on your mudpack. You watched the late TV show; I watched the late TV show; the baby was crying.

During the times I did succeed the activity was not entirely satisfactory for a variety of reasons. On six occasions you chewed gum the whole time; every so often you watched TV the whole time. Frequently you told me to hurry up and get it over with. A few times I tried to awaken you to tell you we were through; and one time I was afraid I had hurt you, for I felt you move.

Honey, it's no wonder I drink too much.

Your Loving Husband

False Piety: Twisting God's Good News

False piety, a behavior that apparently got under Jesus' skin pretty easily, is at the heart of why the church won't embrace legitimate sexual needs and thereby makes it more difficult for intimacy to flourish in Christian marriages.

Piety is devotion and reverence, usually religious, and usually toward God. "False piety" means pretending that you believe something is spiritually valuable, usually through lip service, even though your actions say you don't. For example, Jesus criticized the Pharisees because they claimed to point people toward God and take his commands seriously, while at the same time they often curried favor and lived for personal gain instead. They weren't really pious; they only appeared to be.

False piety tells us not to dialogue or ask about sex because such talk isn't "proper" or "spiritual." Falsely pious Christians eliminate sex when they speak about married intimacy, pretending therein to be making marriage "more holy." This view is mistaken, anti-biblical, and built on lies (sometimes but not always intentional). The Bible devotes an entire book, Song of Songs, to the goodness of sexual union, to physical and emotional intimacy. Song of Songs unabashedly makes the connection between sex and intimacy, a connection frequently lost within our churches and in our culture. Eugene Peterson, who paraphrased Song of Songs from its original and steamy Hebrew language, observes:

> The Song proclaims an integrated wholeness that is at the center of Christian teaching on committed, wedded love for a world that seems to specialize in loveless sex. The Song is a convincing witness that men and women were created physically, emotionally, and spiritually to live in love.[15]

And some of it's not exactly Sunday school material:

- "His head resting between my breasts—the head of my lover."
- "You are tall and supple, like a palm tree, and your full breasts are like sweet clusters of dates. I say 'I'm going to climb that palm tree! Oh yes! Your breasts . . .'" (1:13; 7:9).

People force themselves into playing a lot of tricks to keep false piety alive. Worst of all is when this includes twisting the Bible. Many Christians have grown up believing that the Song of Songs is not as it appears. We've been told that it's not about the celebration of sexual intimacy and pleasure between a married couple—that it's really a metaphor explaining Christ's deep love for his church. (This from a church that leans toward literal interpretation of almost every other biblical section.) Why we would need such a "metaphor" when the entire New Testament attests to this loving relationship has never been well explained.

According to God, Song of Songs is a public document meant to be discussed, and sexuality is a behavior that's meant to be celebrated. However, large parts of the church have denied this, and the allegorization of Song of Songs has been tragic for Nice Guys. A Christian man reads it and finds out that God created and endorses his sexual desires. He finally has a witness, a book, an author, a *King* who understands his heart and his challenge! He finally gets the biggest amen of all—then he's told, "Not so fast. This book doesn't mean anything like what you think it says."

His own subculture doesn't respect or sometimes even rightly acknowledge his nature, his heart, and his passions. Talk about a sucker punch. He feels as though he's supposed to be different, feel different, act different than he is, feels, and does. If he follows suit and tries to suppress himself, against his nature and against God's plan, he's likely to develop anxiety, fear, or depression; temptations toward sexual sin will carry even greater lure if his sexuality's true expression is misdirected.

CNG marriages can't afford to mishandle or ignore this essential element. From a negative perspective, doing so causes disaster and inner death. Positively, though: handling it rightly can be a fundamental building block for intimacy in all manner of areas. *A CNG's desire for sexual closeness is often so strong that it can be a top motivator for him to confront his fear, leave Niceland, become emotionally honest, and be available to you.*

Some of our gender differences are just flat-out amusing. Men produce twice as much saliva and have thicker skulls. (Maybe thicker heads *isn't* so surprising!) Women pause less when talking and are better at tongue twisters.

And then there are the differences that if misunderstood and mishandled can be the difference between marriage and divorce. Merely understanding the facts isn't enough. Our knowledge and wisdom need to go into both our heads *and* hearts, transforming into beliefs, actions, and most important, respect for our differences. This will give him the freedom he needs to change, and you will be giving yourself the peace of mind to rest in your good deeds. You may well see that your problems aren't as unworkable as they appear.

CHAPTER 6

PROCEEDING WITH WISDOM, GRACE, AND LOVE

When you love, you wish to do things for.
You wish to sacrifice for. You wish to serve.[1]
ERNEST HEMINGWAY

Many of us have had a misconception that intimacy is fully synonymous with pleasure, and it can take time for the reality of the larger picture to settle and take hold. Other challenges are in store as well: good, helpful challenges. Like a lot of beneficial ideas, these may appear strange at first. Though you may not be used to hearing them, they have the power to help transform your marriage.

We want to help you proceed with specific ways of wisdom, grace, and love as you take up the task of learning how to approach your

CNG. The cornerstone you're about to embark upon is the necessity of self-reflection, which is intrinsic to moral living and positive change.

This Is *Good* Work, Not Nice

The first thing to note: This work isn't what we usually think of as *nice*. Lynne Hybels, who along with her husband, Bill, helped start Willow Creek Community Church in 1972, wrote about her struggle with being a pleasant Christian in *Nice Girls Don't Change the World*. The opposite of nice girls, she says, is "good girls." A good woman is a "downright dangerous woman. [She is] a woman who shows up with everything she is and joins the battle against whatever opposes the redeeming work of God in our lives and in our world."[2]

God wants your CNG to come out of his cave and pick up the sword he's dropped. He wants to transform your guy into a man of faith, love, courage, and integrity. You may well be the most important person God will use in this mighty work. The enemy of his soul doesn't want this growth to happen—that makes you a dangerous woman indeed. Such women, writes Hybels, think creatively, take risks, reinvent their lives, and follow their God-given dreams. This isn't always nice, but it is always good.

Hybels, an advocate for Africans with HIV/AIDS, concludes with a wise, heartfelt pledge of good-woman living that describes much of the love-filled redemptive work ahead. Pray it into your own soul.

> May we be dangerous women. May we be women who acknowledge our power to change, and grow, and be radically alive in God. May we be healers of wounds and righters of wrongs. May we weep with those who weep and speak for those who cannot speak for themselves. May we cherish children, embrace the elderly, and empower the poor. May we pray deeply and teach wisely. May we be strong and gentle leaders. May we sing songs of joy and talk down fear. May we never hesitate to let passion push us, conviction

propel us, and righteous anger energize us. May we strike fear into all that is unjust and evil in the world. May we dismantle abusive systems and silence lies with truth. May we shine like stars in a darkened generation. May we overflow with goodness in the name of God and by the power of Jesus. And in that name, and by that power, may we change the world.[3]

Have you thought your desire for intimacy was a mere dream, a selfish cause? Not so. Your desire to be close to your man is much more. It may even lead to his spiritual transformation and personal awakening. You transform, too, as you become an agent of redemptive love.

This good work means you are not a doormat for poor behavior. Jesus said, "If your brother wrongs you, reprove him; if he repents, forgive him" (Luke 17:3 NEB). This is very straightforward: You are not a punching bag for the enjoyment, amusement, frustrations, or shortcomings of others. If your CNG wrongs you, do something about it. Let your feelings and thoughts be known, but in a constructive way. The forgiveness that follows his repentance will lighten both your soul and his.

The Meaning of Commitment

One reason people believe they're required to accept (without a word) the poor state of a marriage comes from a misunderstanding of commitment. Commitment means so much more than just sticking together in good times and bad—that often has more to do with endurance.

In regard to marriage, commitment is best understood as the virtue of applying yourself to a task or a goal. Commitment is not a passive pursuit; it doesn't mean just persisting by existing, and it doesn't mean not expressing your concerns. CNGs are experts at "hanging in there," but that's no way to live—for one thing, it profoundly lacks courage, faith, and adventure. With a CNG marriage, "hanging in there" is like a slow leak in a car tire. Pretty soon it's more than useless—it's hazardous.

Commitment is powerful, purposeful, down-to-business living. Commitment seeks out problems before they happen. Commitment anticipates, scans, and confronts in order to create intimacy, not just win an argument.

As we have seen, in Luke 16, Jesus praises shrewdness, ingenuity, and the kind of cunning behavior that leads to redemptive living. His statement that the "people of this world are more shrewd in dealing with their own kind than are the people of the light" (v. 8) does *not* mean this is a good thing. Jesus is encouraging his followers to be more shrewd, not less. As Eugene Peterson renders this powerful truth in *The Message:*

> Streetwise people are smarter in this regard than law-abiding citizens. They are on constant alert, looking for angles, surviving by their wits. I want you to be smart in the same way—but for what is right—using every adversity to stimulate you to creative survival . . . so you'll live, really live, and not complacently just get by on good behavior. (vv. 8–9)

Get it? Proper decorum and grinning faces don't cut it in life, and they certainly don't cut it in marriage. More is required of the truly committed. Christians have been erroneously told that the key to abundant living is found almost exclusively in personal piety. But Jesus never said this, and our lives suffer when we fail to recognize our astonishing lack of balance.

Of *course* our behavior should be upstanding, and of *course* our actions should be beyond reproach. There is nothing synonymous between living rightly and being passive; also, intellect and sound judgment do not contradict cleverness and ingenuity. God gave us our minds—we are to muster the knowledge we have and endeavor to expand it.

There is another truth that you cannot sidestep or ignore. Most forms of passivity result from fear and anxiety, and most overblown fears have at their core a lie that's been ingested and digested. Your actions and words may well lead your CNG to the awareness that lies are holding him captive. You can help cultivate his resulting soul work, walking alongside him, but you can't take over and fight his spiritual battle for him. If you try to rescue him, he won't be able to undergo the changes that he needs to begin, embrace, and maintain.

If you reject this and try to walk his path for him, you will not be a catalyst for change against passivity. When he begins his quest, *help* him through it as he makes decisions and takes steps. If he's looking for options, give suggestions, but then let him make the subsequent decisions, and when he does, support him. Aim to be like a nurse: You can't undergo the sick one's physical healing, but you can serve to create and uphold a healing environment.

I most likely would not have undertaken my spiritual battle against passivity if it weren't for Sandy's help and availability. I fumbled, stumbled, and imperfectly progressed because I wanted to be closer to her and to others, even though I often felt I didn't know how. Sandy likewise fumbled and stumbled

YOU CAN HELP CULTIVATE HIS RESULTING SOUL WORK, WALKING ALONGSIDE HIM, BUT YOU CAN'T TAKE OVER AND FIGHT HIS SPIRITUAL BATTLE FOR HIM.

and imperfectly conveyed her reciprocation of my desire.

We want to help you minimize your stumbling. But also know there will be mistakes. Please don't languish over this—we're human, and we have to cut each other slack, extra when we're climbing the toughest mountains.

Peace-Making vs. Peace-Faking

The Christian subculture has plenty of false peace masquerading as the real thing. In marriage, peace is not one resentful person caving in so as to maintain a form of "harmony" in the home. True, a wise spouse learns to keep the mouth shut regarding behavior that's largely a nuisance or sometimes irritating. That's life. But sweeping genuinely destructive problems under the rug: that is not peace-making, it's peace-faking. If you have kids, peace-faking shows them only the wrong way to resolve conflict. Ultimately, the particular sins associated with passive living will need to be addressed; *there's nothing good about faking peace, and doing so is not submission.*

God's holy word in the hands of a foolish, self-centered person can do immense harm. We've seen a passive-aggressive husband use the Bible to grotesquely dominate his wife. With a smile he shot verses like arrows when she wisely pointed out that his sinful, manipulative control was destroying their home. He stuck to his "head of my household" script and remained disengaged, refusing to embrace honesty or humility. Their marriage didn't survive.

His "headship" was a self-serving form of domination, not assertive, initiating leadership that blesses and strengthens, the qualities found in the New Testament term for "head." (This is the Greek word *kephale*; e.g., see 1 Corinthians 11:3.) That some self-serving spouses have abused this concept doesn't mean the rest of us should throw it out.

God's Word shows that women have a unique corresponding ability and responsibility, a creative counterpart to a man's leadership role. This is found in the Old Testament as the Hebrew term *azar*, meaning "to help" (Genesis 2:18, 20); it's a God-given gift. And it's a gift to a wise husband, if he's humble enough to listen and if it's given without harshness or denigration.

Azar does not mean merely taking and carrying out orders, and it does not signify any lack of significance or directive toward passivity.

The New Testament's call for a woman to exercise her influence as helper is a mandate; rejecting or avoiding it may well be sinful. The New Testament likewise shows a man that he must mature in leadership, loving his wife and trusting God to aid his marriage (Ephesians 5:22, 24, 33; Colossians 3:18; 1 Peter 3:1, 5).

A marriage is created and built between two unique individuals, not between a generic guy unit and a generic gal unit. There is no one who's exactly the same as anyone else—we're not symbols on the doors of public restrooms. A marriage thrives as God intends when each partner lives as a loving and obedient disciple of Christ.

Regarding marriage, the reality of God's love as shown to us in Jesus calls for mutual submission between husband and wife (Ephesians 5:21–33). This rules out domination, inequality, manipulation, intimidation, and general selfishness. The widely cited text about wives submitting to husbands (vv. 22–24) is preceded by commands for each of us to be filled with the Spirit and for mutual submission between one believer and another (vv. 18, 21).

As a partial illustration, it helps to think of the husband as first among equals. Why? The reasons are multifaceted, and it would take another book to explain them in depth. For our purposes, however, one profound reason: part of a married

PART OF A MARRIED MAN'S CHARACTER AND SOUL ATROPHIES AND DIES WHEN HE DOESN'T EXERCISE LEADERSHIP.

man's character and soul atrophies and dies when he doesn't exercise leadership.

Headship has specific borders. It cannot ask you to do things God forbids, and it can't forbid what God commands. Submission does not equate to slavish obedience. You, Christian woman, are a follower of Jesus, equal in worth and value and responsible for your own behavior.

In *God's New Society,* John Stott puts it this way:

> We have to be very careful not to overstate this biblical teaching on authority. It does not mean that the authority of husbands, parents and masters is unlimited, or that wives, children and workers are required to give unconditional obedience. No, the submission required is to God's authority delegated to human beings. If, therefore, they misuse their God-given authority then our duty is no longer conscientiously to submit, but conscientiously to refuse to do so. For to submit in such circumstances would be to disobey God. The principle is clear: we must submit right up to the point where obedience to human authority would involve disobedience to God.[4]

Biblical submission to the truth of God's love means you are required *not* to follow into sin. This can be challenging and confusing for the wife of a passive husband; he is more prone to harder-to-spot sins of omission (failure to do something right) than sins of commission (choosing to do something wrong). Make no mistake about it: The passive lifestyle is a sinful lifestyle. It not only fails to lead, it also fails to love, protect, and be honest. It violates fidelity.

A husband's unwillingness or inability to be proactive often leaves his home susceptible to needless economic pressures. His lack of expressed love makes for confusion, frustration, and felt rejection. A wife doesn't feel valued or cherished. Their children, sensing they don't have a trustworthy man in their corner, feel unprotected and become fearful. The weight of life presses down on their spirits; they lack guardianship and guidance.

You see these realities because you are close to him. You see the sins of omission like no one else does, so others can't entirely affirm your concerns. Don't let this stop you from rightly acting upon them in the ways we've been describing. Do not silently sit by and let destruction continue like it has in this resentful woman's home:

My husband is the perfect Christian Nice Guy. He even calls himself a nice guy. It's like he's proud of it, but when I see what it does in our home it's disgusting. He doesn't stand up for us. He has let people overcharge us for things that he knows aren't right but he won't say anything to them. One of our kids came home from school crying because of a bully and my husband didn't do anything about it. And he doesn't say anything when our kids speak disrespectfully to me. He doesn't believe in financial planning so our finances are also a mess. I could keep going on and on. I'm glad you wrote your book so wives like me don't have to live like this forever.

Note this CNG's many failures to act; he's been systematically sinning by omission. Christian spouses become worse than victims—they can also be accomplices to damage and deterioration through misguided ideas about submission. "The word submission means to align oneself under another person in order to serve a greater good. To submit is to serve the other to help them grow in glory."[5] Niceness grows only destruction. It is incapable of glory.

Questioning action and inaction, and pointing out the error of ways, is not rebellion or disrespect. Sandy did this when she noticed that I would not stand up for myself because I feared conflict and repercussion. It didn't help that I worked for a string of abusive bosses or that I was too frozen by fear to move forward into a better workplace environment. Done with gentleness and right motives, pointing out problems is loving and respectful. Refusing to go along with lack of action and, therefore, recklessness, is not sin. Do not take a front-row seat to domestic damage. Passively sitting back and watching destruction unfold is not the "will of the Lord," it's fatalism.

What Dance Lessons *Really* Taught Us

As mentioned earlier, we've been taking dance lessons. Finally. We don't know why it took so many years for us to get started. Perhaps we weren't ready to push aside our fear of public mistakes. Maybe we weren't ready for such a practical demonstration of leadership and support. Anyway, we're in it, and we're still beginners, so if you meet us, please don't ask us to demonstrate.

The Argentine tango is by far the most stunning dance of the three we've begun to learn. It shows us what couples are able to accomplish through defined roles. These parameters, properly executed, give the impression that there are no parameters. It's not obvious that anyone is leading or supporting. The fruit of this is delicious.

What you see is two people mustering their talent, power, and sensuality to create their own unique form of physical and emotional intimacy that neither one's movement could create alone. He steps forth and leads with intention; she supports his intention, enhancing their shared desire to make something grand. He leans into her, and she into him.

There is no script. They move by the impulses of their hearts, by the room's physical borders, around others in their path. As in life, they ad lib; accordingly, someone has to lead, or they will crash together. Otherwise, it'd just be a matter of time before everyone on the dance floor was on the floor.

Her support has no degradation. She glows with dignity. She honors him.

His lead is not stern or overbearing. He exudes reverence. He cherishes her.

One does not fall into the sin of domination; the other doesn't cower and in so doing become an accomplice. If they did, it would be heartbreaking to witness. He pushing her around the floor and scowling; she retaliating with spiteful words and punitive glares. An act with so much potential for beauty would become a foul display, just another gender-war skirmish and more intimacy potential lost. It would be like watching an anti-miracle—wine turned into tap water.

After our friends Rick and Barb finish demonstrating a dance move,

I (Paul) have no inclination to go up and say, "Rick, great job in your leadership capacity. Barb, you're so subservient to him." Any guy who'd want to say such a thing would be seeing what he wants to see and missing the entire point. The main issue isn't who does what just for the sake of doing it; it's what they create together. What we're meant to notice isn't someone leading and someone supporting. Two people creating beauty together is both humbling and exciting.

When done well, it's a powerful, graceful, permeating, intimate creation of gender harmony. With interlocking wills, both bring their talent, courage, respect, and desire to work together.

Be Careful With "Spiritual Leadership"

Remember the differences between being passive and being reserved? Take note: Some Christian wives incorrectly believe their husband is passive in not behaving like their outgoing pastor, or like another man they admire who more naturally embraces an out-front leadership role. Specifically, these women have a narrow view of spiritual leadership out of line with what we find in the Bible.

Not everyone is called to be a preacher—that takes particular skills. And not everyone is a skilled teacher. Some are outgoing like the apostles Peter and Paul; the spiritual leadership of others is more understated, behind the scenes. Don't try to stuff your husband into an unfair and unwarranted leadership model; it won't help your marriage, and it's likely to send him underground.

When we first married, Sandy expected me to lead in mutual Bible study. We attended a church that claimed it is the husband's responsibility to illuminate the Scriptures to his wife, heavily insinuating that wives aren't capable of extensive biblical understanding without a husband's aid. I strongly disagreed, maintaining that this isn't the husband's place but rather the Spirit's. A spouse does have influence over what the other thinks; that's *not* the same as seeing yourself as a kind of oracle in his or her life.

I eventually conceded and led a study with Sandy. It would be among the most painful experiences of my married life, an agonizing endeavor that sent me to new lows in CNG living.

After I finished reading and teaching from John's gospel, Sandy sat dumbfounded. After an intense, silent pause, she said, "That's not how my pastor taught it."

Who are you, Satan?! I wondered. I was tempted to search her forehead for "666." To a man reluctant to lead in the first place, this was like a spear through my heart. I couldn't win if I didn't lead, and I was shot down when I did.

This is an all-too-common experience. CNGs don't garner the respect of their wives because people don't respect those who are fearful and reluctant. We train others in how to treat us. CNGs train others to treat them poorly. When they do make a rare appearance at life's home plate, bat in hand, ready to swing, they're often met with a series of inside fastballs—some of which hit them, knock them down, and leave them with concussed souls.

David Murrow, author of *Why Men Hate Going to Church,* says Christian men are often forced into roles thrust upon them by others, especially when it comes to being a father. His words should factor into our consideration of spiritual leadership:

> Most kids when they are older don't remember what was said during family devotions. But they remember with intense clarity the feeling they got when their dad took them fishing or did other outdoor pursuits. That kind of love stays with them forever.[6]

Family devotions weren't much fun for us either at first. Sandy had set beliefs as to how they should be conducted and how they should be taken from certain books and particular sermons. She expected me to be a preacher; I'm really more skilled as a teacher. To me, preaching to your children is a surefire way to make them rebel. I prefer teaching them— for example, asking intentional questions about a passage or story, or playing the devil's advocate—to better help them grow their faith. It took time for Sandy to accept, respect, and, at last, appreciate this different approach.

Sandy struggled with what she now sees as a cookie-cutter shape for spiritual leadership; she knows that the way she protested and questioned seemed undermining, and it pushed me away. I struggled with staying true to what I believed—being consistent and authentic while becoming expressive and engaged. Sandy learned to give me room to be myself; as I felt more supported, I was more confident and involved, which formed deeper respect in her and gave her a sense of protection.

We don't share this to make either of us look like a monster or a victim. Those days are over. We want you to know how to avoid "well-meaning destruction." The general principle: Loan your man your respect when he tries to be more assertive, and broaden your understanding of spiritual leadership to include other applications of it.

You Win, Regardless

Are you having doubts about whether *anything* can truly serve to form and sustain intimacy in your marriage? Are you wondering whether we're guaranteeing success? How we wish we could tell you with complete certainty that everything will go off for you without a hitch. But there are already many books sold on the rubble of others' broken dreams. The fact is, every couple's progress will be unique. Many factors influence and impact the results, and one of the biggest is that you can't control another person's life. You really can't make him do something he doesn't want to do—at least for very long.

We want to encourage you to persist with this important work anyway, even though it's possible that not everything will transpire as wished. Why would a woman in her right mind take up this endeavor without some assurance that it's going to succeed? For one thing, because you've already been committing such acts of bravery all your life. Laboring for what you want and what you believe is liberating, giving the peaceful assurance that you know you are giving your all, doing your best. *Your pursuit of intimacy will grow you and make you a victor no matter what anyone else ever chooses.*

We constantly embark upon risky adventures with no victory guarantee. We study subjects we can flunk. We pour phenomenal energy and hope into jobs without knowing if we'll keep them. We marry with no concrete certainty of fidelity. We have children without being sure they will outlive us or won't crush our hearts. If we let fear—fear of failure, disappointment, tragedy, or loss—freeze our feet and harden our hearts, we shrivel and become small, joyless, bitter, petty, jaded. Loveless.

> **YOUR PURSUIT OF INTIMACY WILL GROW YOU AND MAKE YOU A VICTOR NO MATTER WHAT ANYONE ELSE EVER CHOOSES.**

We're willing to learn new skills to keep a job that will never love us back; why should we let fear of the unknown halt us from redemptive work in marriage? While the answers are many, at the top is this: We are part of a culture that doesn't rightly value love and intimacy. We chafe at the prospect of investing in relationship with no guarantee of reward. The problem with this is that love and intimacy cannot be commanded or bargained. They can only be given and received. *Love and intimacy are an offering.*

A culture that valued love and intimacy would teach its children about love and intimacy's need for *time*.

It would teach the difference between "in love" and loving; it would impart to its members the value of the mutuality on which their lives depend. A culture versed in the workings of emotional life would encourage and promote the activities that sustain health—togetherness with one's partner and children; homes, families, and communities of connectedness. Such a society would guide its inhabitants to the joy that can be found at the heart of attachment. . . .

The contrast between that culture and our own could not be more evident. . . . Top-ranking items [in our culture] remain the pursuit of wealth, physical beauty, youthful appearance, and the shifting, elusive markers of status. There are brief spasms of pleasure to be had at the end of those pursuits—the razor-thin delight of the latest purchase, the momentary glee of flaunting this promotion or that unnecessary trinket—pleasures here, but no contentment.[7]

Part of your success is acknowledging that the culture isn't going to help you obtain something it undervalues. You may even have family members and girlfriends who will try to convince you that it's a waste of time, that you could do so much better, that he won't change. But they don't know this, and neither do you. God frequently arranges changes that can only be fully understood and appreciated in hindsight. His timing is often not ours.

Our society is primarily concerned with success through competition, leaving little appreciation or room for our hearts. Instead of contentment with our vast success as viewed in the light of human history, we are trained in the ways of discontentment. When surveyed, Americans rank among the world's lowest in regard to happiness. We live as though success is measured first in material gain; as a result, respect in America is obtained primarily by being either famous or wealthy. Passive or not, most men obtain neither, and widespread respect for them is fleeting at best.

American males are trained to be efficient, not known. Sharing hearts and creating intimacy doesn't get you ahead in a competitive and shifting market. He lives most of his time in a work environment where showing his emotions is detrimental and where family values are at log-gerheads with other priorities. We may talk a lot about family values, but in the end he knows that reading to his kids Sunday night will not prepare him for handling Monday's big meeting.

AMERICAN MALES ARE TRAINED TO BE EFFICIENT, NOT KNOWN.

When I interviewed Frank Abagnale Jr., subject of the book and movie *Catch Me If You Can*, I asked Frank what made him change his criminal ways. Frank wished he could say he saw the light or had a personal epiphany. What really happened? He met a good woman and he wanted her to be proud of him. Her love transformed him.

Philip Yancey writes about a similar transformation at the hands of "Woman." *You* possess an age-old power, as old as romance herself, as old as redemption. It's a God-given power, yours to spend, keep, or mis-spend. The question is, what will you do with your heroic potential?

Why give your heart to this? Because intimacy is deeply beneficial to both of you and to your children. There may be a rich reward waiting for you. Deep, abiding attachment makes you more healthy and vital, more resilient against life's many stresses. Two, glued with love and inti-macy, are much stronger than one.

Why should you try? Because you are connected to this man. He is part of your life. Even as you may have tried to distance yourself from him, your soul is affected. "A couple shares in one process, one dance, one story. Whatever improves that one benefits both; whatever detracts hurts and weakens both lives."[8]

Why keep going when reason may be telling you to stop? Because "reason's last step," wrote Blaise Pascal, "is recognizing that an infinity of things surpass it."[9] Pascal, one of the most brilliant men history has known, spent much of his life exploring reason. Reason is powerful and important. People make huge mistakes when they live without or in denial of it. But we also make huge mistakes when we make it more than it is. Love and intimacy surpass reason.

You are discontented. Discontent takes its toll—it grows unless it's actively opposed. It leads to thoughts of infidelity, and we're not just talking adultery. It's human nature to break faith with those we don't respect. Our hearts wander, slippery at first, emboldened later, until we start dreaming of new domestic landscapes, a new home life with a new partner. This delicious seduction needs to be supplanted with new eyes, a refreshed mind, and a cleansed heart.

Changing your approach toward your CNG will bring you relief from daydreams of escape. It will bring him relief from all kinds of pressure that not only don't work but push him further into the passive lifestyle. If you have children, you will be helping to create more harmony and security for them. You will also be modeling assertiveness, one of the healthiest qualities they can learn in seeing how to avoid disaster and divorce in the future.

Spiritual growth awaits you, regardless of what your husband does. You will be stronger, wiser, more trained in the ways of love if you keep going. You will be a better equipped redemptive force for good in this messed-up world. You will be more like Jesus. You will have fought a good fight, whether or not the fruit of your labor is instantly or quickly apparent.

There is no failure when one person grows and matures. Heroes are heroic not always because they succeed but because they are willing to try. Surely you've noticed how many ultimately settle for boring mediocrity in marriage? By embracing this path, you will have shown that you aren't willing to accept something just because it's common or status quo. You know there's more, and rather than saying "I deserve it," you'll be saying "I'm willing to find it, learn it, and live it."

CHAPTER 7

HANDLING ISSUES OF ANGER, RESPECT, AND RESENTMENT

You can be right, but wrong at the top of your voice.[1]

EMERSON EGGERICHS

O f the negative and unpleasant emotions and other responses that go through the upset mind of a CNG wife, three of the biggest are anger, dwindling respect, and resentment. Like mishandled gender differences, all three don't just hinder your chances at intimacy—they stop it dead in its tracks. They create discontent and desperate housewives, women who, tentatively, then cautiously, then curiously, then perhaps actively dream about and consider being with a new partner. We want to help you see that you don't need a new partner. New eyes can help you to clearly and fairly see your CNG and spur your heart on to taking up the sacred work of facilitating healing.

Expectations and Anger

American women in general and American Christian wives in particular have been given not-quite-right information about what husbands (passive or not) are going to do for them. Generally, when their expectations are unfulfilled, they feel misled. Gradually and increasingly, they feel hurt, and they feel angry.

The emotion of anger is so valuable when handled properly and so destructive when handled improperly (more common). Some of the anger you face is the result of false expectations and feeling like you have no control, leaving you with the sinking *feeling* of powerlessness. The sense of having no strength can gradually turn anger into rage; however, the powerlessness you may feel isn't accurate. Again, you have far more power than you realize.

Whether or not he's a passive man whose heart is still controlled by fear rather than governed by love, the expectation that he will be constantly romantic and emotionally connected is unrealistic for a man who holds down a regular job in a fluctuating and unreliable market. In most vocational settings it's detrimental to show real feelings. Men must hold private thoughts inside as they go through workplace cycles where expressing true emotions could hurt them. For forty or more weekly hours, male authenticity often simply isn't an option (not even accounting for time spent commuting or handling work elements outside of actual work time).

Most men have been forced to compartmentalize their emotional world. They have already mastered the repression of their feelings in other spheres; it's naturally a challenge and a struggle to learn how to (and be willing to) release them at home. Few men do this well, especially early in marriage, and CNGs, in their current state, are especially limited in emotional flexibility, so the tension between what's effective at work and at home is even greater.

It takes most men years to figure out how to leave work behind and give you and the children the attention he wants and needs to give. For most, it's a learned lifestyle whose process is messy—some steps forward, some back. You can help to ensure that he has room to make mistakes as he grows. If much or most of what he hears from you, directly or indirectly, is that he's a romantic dud and a spiritual failure, you will be trying to build a bond of attachment from a platform of antagonism.

ANOTHER VIEW OF SPIRITUAL LEADERSHIP

by **DAVID MURROW**, author of *Why Men Hate Going to Church*

Men are all about competence and being successful. Faced with the possibility of failure, a man will often bow and go passive.

Think about men in their role as "spiritual leaders of their home." How likely are they to succeed? As we currently define that term, not very likely. And it has nothing to do with a man's faith. Biologically, psychologically and socially, men are poorly equipped to be "spiritual leaders" as we currently understand that term. We need a better definition of spiritual leadership. Here's why.

First, a spiritual leader is [supposed to be] a good reader. He must be in God's Word daily, read Christian books and literature, and be able to read aloud to his family from devotionals. But men are often poor readers. Men are diagnosed with reading disorders at four times the rate of women. The Department of Education's National Assessment of Adult Literacy reported that over the past decade, women gained literacy skills while men headed in the opposite direction. A large percentage of U.S. men never pick up another book after high school.

Second, a spiritual leader is [supposed to be] good at praying aloud. He leads his children in mealtime and bedtime prayers, and prays aloud with his wife. But this is tough for a lot of guys. The verbal regions of a man's brain are smaller than the corresponding regions in a woman's brain. . . .

Third, men are competitive. Men may see themselves competing with their wives or the preacher in these areas. "I just can't pray like Pastor George, so I don't even try," said one man I know. "My wife can pray for hours at a time, but all I can muster is, 'God, thank you for this day.' I feel like such a loser when I try to pray out loud," said another.

We need an expanded definition of "spiritual leader."

As I look at the ministry of Jesus and the disciples, I don't see a lot of reading, study, and discussion. Without question, Jesus knew the Scriptures inside and out, and he'd obviously studied them extensively. But the emphasis of the Gospels is on living out the Word, not necessarily talking about it. The primary issue isn't whether a man comes to be a master scholar; what's critical is that he comes to see every moment of life as an opportunity to lead his family. As Moses said to Israel:

> These commandments that I give you today are to be upon your hearts. Impress them on your children. Talk about them when you sit at home and when you walk along the road, when you lie down and when you get up. Tie them as symbols on your hands and bind them on your foreheads. Write them on the doorframes of your houses and on your gates. (Deuteronomy 6:6–9)

Being a spiritual leader isn't always a book-on-the-lap experience. It's to be woven into the fabric of everyday life. Each trip to the hardware store, each drive home after a baseball game, each tickle fight is an opportunity to point children to the reality of God's presence and work in their lives. You can help your man become this kind of leader. If he's not comfortable leading family devotions or bedtime prayers, encourage him instead in these areas:

- Spending time with the kids—*being* with them.
- Taking you out for coffee or dinner or ice cream, even when there's no agenda.
- Talking with the kids about his experiences growing up, or situations where he had to choose between right and wrong.
- Establishing a regular time when he tells you about his day.

Most men have no idea how much "spiritual leadership" comes simply from kind words, noticing little things, spending time with those he loves. Encourage your man to lead in a way that feels real— not necessarily religious—to him.

The state that most men long to experience in their home is *tranquility*. Here are two broad ways in which you can begin to create that state: (1) learn to embrace legitimate expecta-

> **THE STATE THAT MOST MEN LONG TO EXPERIENCE IN THEIR HOME IS *TRANQUILITY*.**

tions—this takes into account that he's a sinner like you and everyone else—and (2) learn to reject illegitimate expectations, one of which is that he will see the world through female eyes.

Recipe for Resentment

It takes a remarkably mature and confident man to hold his ground and speak the truth in love. Instead of confronting false expectations, many men escape, either inside or outside the home. When this makes matters worse, many women pursue and pressure; when he further flees and recedes, she feels even more spurned, deprived, and powerless.

This is where undercutting begins. Resentment starts to supersede respect. Behind his back, she speaks badly of him to girlfriends and family, sometimes to his friends or colleagues. She may cut him off sexually, even try to turn their own children against him.

This is one reason I launched my Good Guy Rebellion. Christians must contend with and combat well-intended but dangerous and false messages that emanate primarily from within the church. Writes Dr. James Dobson:

> No one should be expected to carry another person emotionally. . . . A good marriage is one in which the dominant needs are met within the relationship, but where each spouse develops individual identity, interests, and friendships. This may be the most delicate tightrope act in marriage. Extreme independence is as destructive to a relationship as total dependence."[2]

Angela Thomas notes:

> In the effort to make things perfect, a woman can beg her man to be like [other perfect men who don't exist]. She's hoping that if he could change, then she'd finally be whole. When the man feels like he is asked to be something he wasn't ever made to be, when he senses the pressure to meet expectations that seem unattainable . . . the man [may] step back in frustration.[3]

That man's wife often then steps up in anger.

Dobson likewise warns against men being saddled with unrealistic expectation:

> Any sadness or depression that a woman might encounter is her husband's fault. At least, [she thinks,] he has the power to eradicate it if he cares enough. In other words, many American women come into marriage with unrealistically romantic expectations, which are certain to be dashed. Not only does this orientation set up a bride

for disappointment and agitation in the future, it also places enormous pressure on her husband to deliver the impossible.[4]

It's challenging enough to meet realistic expectations in any marriage. Unrealistic expectations in CNG marriages only make matters worse.

ON BEING WISE AS A SERPENT

Think long and hard before you speak poorly about your husband to anyone. It's one thing to share your concerns; it's another to denigrate him in front of others. Additionally, thinking that repeatedly complaining about the same problems will make them go away is much like beating your head against a wall in trying to create a door. Don't add difficulties onto difficulties; instead, determine to work toward solutions.

CNG Marriages and Domestic Violence

Most people assume that men are almost always more violent, and men are sometimes seen as the only ones who need help with anger and the sources of anger. In reality, both genders need help. Spousal abuse from wife to husband is currently an underreported problem in the homes of passive men.

Domestic-violence research overwhelmingly shows that women are as likely as men to initiate and engage in domestic violence, and that much of female domestic violence is not committed in self-defense. Studies show that women often compensate for smaller size by greater use of weapons and the element of surprise.[5]

According to Phil Cook, author of *Abused Men—The Hidden Side of Domestic Violence,* one "study found a slight but statistically significant rate of greater severe violence by women against their husbands" in strongly religious homes. "Anecdotal evidence suggests that the violence may be a result of the failure of the men to adhere" to traditional leadership inside and outside the home, part of the definition of the CNG lifestyle. Commonly, in specific situations, "the woman lets the husband take the lead role, but if the man fails to be as assertive as she wishes, at home and in private, she becomes violent."[6]

In a highly publicized and very sad 2005 case, a prominent Christian speaker and author faced domestic violence charges for assaulting her husband. Police reports documented that while having an argument in their car, they pulled off to the side of the road. According to at least four witnesses, when he got out and started to walk away, she grabbed him by the throat and choked him. He broke free, ran to a parking lot, and concealed himself behind a furniture truck. She pursued him into the parking lot with her car.

If a man committed the same actions—even if the charges were alleged rather than in front of several eyewitnesses—he would be denounced and blackballed. As it stands today, most people have a hard time believing such abuse could be perpetrated by a woman. Some don't believe it, and many assume that this man must have said something to "deserve it."

Official Department of Justice statistics show that men commit 70 percent of all murder of intimates (women, 30 percent). When other factors are accounted for, including unsolved murders, poisonings mistakenly classified as heart attacks, and contract killings classified as "multiple-offender killings," women are almost as likely as men to murder their current or former spouses or intimates.[7]

If a *child* is physically abused in his home, it is more likely to come at the hand of his mother than his father. Some studies suggest that the rate is as high as 63 percent.[8]

We receive CNG letters like this one:

My wife hits me and yells at me and tells me I deserve it. She says horrible things about me in front of our boys. She says that I don't stand up like a man should and she beats me up and taunts me to hit her back.

Why does our culture widely choose either to pretend this isn't happening or to excuse it by explaining it away? Regardless, the fact is, many wives in CNG marriages feel caught in a revolving cycle of anger, shame, and humiliation. Some commit abuse and violence against their husbands.

When the anger of a CNG wife is out of control, she feels ashamed about what she's done. Shame will not heal her or grow her; the wrongs need to come into the light, where the issues can be put into perspective and the couple can receive the help they need, seeking forgiveness and embarking on the path toward reconciliation. Golda Meir said, "You cannot shake hands with a clenched fist."

There is no excuse for abuse. Every person is responsible for what he or she does and says; anything you have done or said in sin is yours to confess and address. If you are in this place and have felt alone, we hope that you are coming to see that you are not—this isn't a rare scenario, and it isn't anywhere outside the realm of what we fallen people can do or say when we don't rightly handle our emotions.

Owning your own behavior also means taking control of what you have control over (which *doesn't* include that man of yours). For me (Sandy) this meant putting down my verbal rolling pin and refusing to use God as my hit-man against Paul. Subsequently, for Paul, it meant seeing and repenting of the damage that passivity and disengagement had been doing to our marriage.

In the years to come, we can expect to see a growing spotlight on this underreported problem that batters domestic harmony and marital intimacy. Just as standing with your hands in your pockets is not an expression of love, neither is berating, belittling, or beating. For most of us, disrespect alone feels like a punch.

Respect: Not Optional

The New Testament gives straightforward direction on creating an intimate, God-glorifying marriage: husbands, love your wives; wives, respect your husbands. That the church needs to emphasize both is a central premise of Emerson Eggerichs' groundbreaking *Love & Respect: The Love She Most Desires, The Respect He Desperately Needs.*

Respect is a vital component to a married man's well-being. It's difficult for even the most mature wife to respect a passive husband, especially if she herself doesn't struggle with passivity. And since passive men don't love well, it's very hard for a CNG to give his wife what most women say they want from a marriage: the feeling that they are cherished.

Men who are in touch with (not consumed by) their emotions are more attractive to women than those who are emotionally flat. Here's a note from a CNG that makes this point only too well:

> I am currently separated from my wife and one of the reasons is because she says that I am not an outgoing person like she thought I was. I don't excite her the way other men can. I hope we get back together.

"Without respect," writes Eggerichs,

> men react to their wives without love. They react as opposed to really talking and reaching consensus during the inevitable disagreements of marriage. As you know, his life is full of reacting to events and opportunities as opposed to level-headed considerations about fundamental parts of his life.[9]

Respect toward your husband, according to God (Ephesians 5:33), is to be unconditional, just as his love toward you is to be unconditional. There is no justification for a husband to say, "I will love my wife *after* she respects me," or for a wife to say, "I will respect my husband *after* he loves me." Or, we must add, *after* your CNG becomes less fearful and passive.

The apostle Peter also gives profound insight into how vital respect is to marriage. He says that if any husbands are disobedient to God's Word, "they may be won without a word by the behavior of their wives, as they observe your chaste and *respectful* behavior" (1 Peter 3:1–2, italics added). Eggerichs says, "Peter is not calling on wives to feel respect; he is commanding them to show respectful behavior. This is not about the husband deserving respect; it is about the wife being willing to treat her husband respectfully *without conditions.*"[10]

> No husband feels affection toward a wife who appears to have contempt for who he is as a human being. . . . When a wife flatly says her husband will have to earn her respect before she gives him any, she leaves the husband in a lose-lose situation. Now he's responsible for both love and respect in the relationship. He must unconditionally love his wife and he also must earn her respect. Is it any wonder he shuts down in the face of all that?[11]

Just how important is respect to a man's self-worth? In a national survey, four hundred men were given a choice: Be left alone and unloved in the world, or feel inadequate and disrespected by everyone. Faced with one or the other, 74 percent said they'd rather be alone and unloved.[12]

Have you ever had someone adamantly disagree with you, stick to her guns, become neither abusive nor passive, and yet leave you with your dignity and honor, even though you lost the argument? I (Paul) had a female boss who did this for me, and it was a real eye-opener. Notice

I didn't write that she did this *to* me. That's because it wasn't an attack—it was an education, fruitful in result and beneficial to experience. Such a woman knows how to respect someone, even when that someone is wrong. She didn't lie and pretend something was right when it wasn't; she spoke her mind without belittling. I felt *energized* afterward because I had a clearer road map to follow, and the quality of my work went up.

Unconditional respect does not mean unconditional acceptance of behavior. Your unconditional respect for him doesn't give your husband the green light to persist in irresponsibility or disengagement in your marriage. It will give him more reason and motivation to step out of his CNG straitjacket.

I have been a coach for nearly a decade. During that time, I can't recall one disrespectful argument with a father; I have had a few with mothers. This doesn't mean I haven't had disagreements with fathers. It's that most men know how to leave another man's dignity intact during conflict. It's like an unspoken bond between guys, and most males learned it on the playgrounds of their youth.

I have said to myself, while being verbally shredded by an angry mother, *Lady, you are so fortunate you're not a man. And I'm so fortunate I'm not married to you.* Most men would rarely tolerate such treatment from another guy, but when they get it from a woman, sometimes they don't feel they have another option. *Part of being a guy,* a man might say to himself, but afterward he wants nothing to do with this kind of woman because he feels so violated with disrespect and hostility.

Disrespect and Adulterous Thinking

Wives are not as averse to adultery as we often believe. There are almost as many unfaithful wives as unfaithful husbands; research generally finds that for every five unfaithful husbands, there are four unfaithful wives.[13] If one were to approach the anatomy of adultery like that of an autopsy, one would find the cancers of disrespect and discontentment throughout the affairs. CNG wives rank high on the emotional Richter scale of both; you *must* be on guard against a wandering heart.

According to Dr. Dobson, such wives feel lonely. They are critical of their husbands for not meeting their needs, for failing to make them feel satisfied and cherished. They are vulnerable to men who show interest in them.

He appears to be far more worthy of respect than her husband; she hasn't felt this alive in a long time. As sexual encounters occur, spiritual life gradually deteriorates. "She rationalizes and lives a double standard. . . . She loses all sexual interest in her husband." When confronted, she is likely either to reconcile or separate. "Such a woman may pity her mate and desire not to hurt him, but she finds him boring and disdainful. . . . A woman wants a man she can look up to, but one who won't look down on her."[14]

Another Side to Resentment

If you've been in the church for a while, you've probably heard plenty about the importance of turning from resentment. It shrinks your soul and harms your body. Writes Joan Lunden: "Holding on to resentment . . . only gives you tense muscles, a headache and a sore jaw from clenching your teeth. Forgiveness gives you back the laughter and the lightness in your life."[15]

> **RESENTMENT IS LIKE DRINKING A GLASS OF POISON AND THEN GLARING AT YOUR OFFENDER AS YOU WAIT FOR HIM TO DIE.**

Resentment is like drinking a glass of poison and then glaring at your offender as you wait for him to die. Resentment is self-destructive, which is another reason we must forgive—we have no more right to harm ourselves than to harm anyone else made in God's image.

It's not that the other person didn't do something wrong. It's that if we aren't careful, their wrong can take ownership of our hearts and minds. In a very real way, resentment allows another to own part of you. Resentment can become an obsession, stealing your joy and ability to see clearly. When it comes to your marriage, you need all the clarity you can get. The call to forgive is also a path to your own freedom.

A message you aren't likely to hear in church is how to avoid feeling resentful in the first place. It's no coincidence that resentment haunts CNG wives: their husbands are more troubling in their behavior, and Christian wives often have been encouraged to leave themselves open to bad spousal behavior.

Resentment must be battled on two fronts: exhuming what's currently in an angry heart, and stemming future openings for resentment to take residence in the heart. This is done by creating healthy boundaries with your spouse to curtail the destruction that comes from passive living. Boundaries prevent (1) cynicism and excessive skepticism, which make rigid boundaries that restrict resolution and intimacy, and (2) näiveté, which makes thin boundaries that lead to further anger and resentment.

Your Secret Weapon: Empathy

How can you exhume resentment and in the process regain respect? *Empathy.* Remember: He doesn't yet see and know the extent of his disengagement. Fearful living is tough. I (Paul) saw fear destroy part of my mother's life, and while nothing excused her behavior, my knowing what fear does to someone made it more understandable and less personal. Empathy is liberating.

Comprehending why someone behaves poorly helps remove the

stinger. When this awareness has time to sink in, you come to realize, as I did, that the problems consuming the one who drives you crazy *aren't about you*. They aren't your fault, so you can quit carrying the other's shame. Said Henry Wadsworth Longfellow: "If we could read the secret history of our enemies, we should find in each man's life sorrow and suffering enough to disarm any hostility."

When I helped one struggling CNG through a tough time with his assertive and abusive wife, he assessed that, despite her cutting tongue, she was a wife of goodwill toward her husband and that she possessed humility. She wanted their relationship to improve and was willing to change if needed; like her husband, she just didn't know what to do next, and at times her frustration got the best of her. I explained to the husband that what she most likely wanted was for him to open up more with her—a scary thought for him, since she sometimes blasted him when he did. He would go into hiding, which made her feel shunned, angry, and resentful. (She needed to learn how to be more respectful and empathetic.) The cycle had been spinning further into trouble.

The husband was so unhappy that I worried he was thinking of getting out. I reminded him that he would need to learn how to be more assertive no matter who he was married to; assertiveness was a skill he needed to obtain regardless. He was finally honest with how he felt. Fireworks flew, so much so they figured it was best to see a marriage counselor for help sorting out their feelings and giving them hope for a better future.

She gave him more room to think, speak, and feel. He felt less pressure, which bolstered his teetering courage. Neither behaved perfectly. It was painful and uncomfortable for both. Yet they showed bravery by addressing their darker sides. I'm glad to report that they're doing very well today.

Some women who read *No More Christian Nice Guy* show Paul

profound empathy and compassion for what he endured as a kid. When they tell him their husband is a CNG, he asks, "Do you think he went through something similar?" Many had never considered the possibility. Some don't want to consider it—you can see it on their face. They are resentful, and they don't want to stop resenting. What they don't realize is that they're going against what they really want.

> **WHAT HAS THAT MAN OF YOURS HAD TO WALK THROUGH? WHAT'S MADE HIM FEEL SMALL, WORTHLESS, POWERLESS? WHAT HAS SO WOUNDED AND FRIGHTENED HIM THAT IT HAS COMPELLED HIM TO LAY DOWN THE SWORD OF HIS WILL?**

Please take a moment to think about this: What has that man of yours had to walk through? What's made him feel small, worthless, powerless? What has so wounded and frightened him that it has compelled him to lay down the sword of his will? This helped soften Sandy's heart, and there's a good chance that your heart will also need to soften before intimacy can grow.

Self-reflection is foundational for living a moral life. Self-reflection should bring you to a deeper understanding of how we tend to see the sins of others more readily than our own—especially when someone hurts us. Jesus addressed this profound tendency when he warned us to see the log in our own eye before trying to take the speck out of another's (Matthew 7:3–5). It's very likely that your response to your husband's passive nature is not without sin.

At the same time, this doesn't mean you excuse his passive behavior, or call it good when it's not. Only make sure you don't condemn him for who he is; you *don't* want him to remain in hiding from you. People who condemn others are basement people, and others aren't attracted to them. When you address your anger, your dwindling respect, and your resentment, you become a balcony person in your man's life. Balcony people draw others toward them.

The Danger of Absolute Straightforwardness

No frank discussion about all these feelings is complete without addressing one more area. There may be one other feeling bothering you. You may not be able to give it a name. Or maybe you can, and you don't think it's right to feel this way. You feel your personal integrity, your self-respect, has gone out the window. You feel . . . embarrassed. *How did I end up marrying a guy like this?*

You worry that your friends and family think he's not good for you, that you could have done better. We recommend that if you possess this feeling of painful self-consciousness, keep it to yourself. Telling him would probably crush his already downtrodden spirit.

To some this advice sounds un-Christian, but listen to this wise counsel from respected marriage counselor Jean Lush. "I hate to see absolute honesty in marriage," she told Dr. Dobson, who asked her to explain exactly what she meant.

Well, let's consider what happens to a woman throughout the menstrual cycle. She can have some pretty depressing days, especially during the premenstrual stage. Speaking personally, I had a very biting vicious tongue at that time, and that is not unusual. Now, if a woman believes she has a right—even an obligation—to be totally honest even when she knows her perception is distorted, she can say some horrid things that she doesn't really mean. That can be very hard on a marriage.

It is simply not healthy to dump all the ugliness on your partner. We need to exercise some discipline in what we say to one another. . . . We don't have to verbalize every thought that comes in our heads. Love is a delicate flower that must be nurtured.[16]

Your embarrassment may be connected with distorted thinking, as Lush mentions. For one thing, there is the matter of *why* your CNG is passive—when all the factors of his life are placed in the mix, passive living is a logical outcome. For another, remember that gender differences can distort our thinking about relationships. Through female glasses, male behavior looks a certain way, and sometimes what seems wrong may be simply different. Men often need far more understanding than fixing.

Embarrassment doesn't make you weird, bad, or rare. At the same time you don't want to be naïve about it either. Express it, but only to God. Give it to him, along with your anger, resentment, and dwindling respect. Ask him to show you creative, loving ways you can help your husband. Ask him to help you soften your heart toward him, to help you become his ally.

Conclusion

How we wish there were a quick prayer that would rid our hearts and minds of what we don't want there. But that has more to do with magic than communion with God, with receiving his power and healing. When you think about it, how would we mature spiritually if our ailments were simply lifted from us? There's no way around spiritual maturity; growth is often borne through the minister of discomfort. As Dr. John Townsend said on Paul's show, "God isn't interested in our comfort. He's interested in our growth." If comfort alone is the reason you became a Christian, you're playing footsy with religion. God has so much more for you.

At its best, intimacy is a level of connected awareness in which two people lift each other up higher than they could go on their own. Much anger, and all resentment and disrespect, hinder intimacy's growth, just as they stunt the other qualities and virtues you want in your marriage. It's time to call a much needed and belated truce.

CHAPTER 8

GOODWILL, ILL WILL: HOW TO TELL

Fools mock at making amends for sin,
but goodwill is found among the upright.

PROVERBS 14:9

Everyone is guilty of all the good he didn't do.

VOLTAIRE

Goodwill is the Rodney Dangerfield of words: it doesn't get the respect it deserves, especially in a culture that undervalues closeness and connection. Goodwill is among the most tangible ways of expressing love and fostering intimacy, yet when we bring images of the word to mind, we think of used clothing. It's time to understand and sing the praises of *the will to do good*, a basic building block for intimacy and so much more than the absence of bad feelings.

Goodwill: It's What's Present, Not Absent

Goodwill is a tangible, practical expression of love. Helpfulness, concern, care, friendly disposition—all related to this workhorse of intimacy—are not the deepest and most philosophical expression of love, but they are pragmatic blessings that make the world (and intimacy with your CNG) go round.

Goodwill is the willingness to act in a spirit of cooperation, not trying to win arguments, where one will stands in stark contrast to another will. It aims to forge the Third Path to the Land of Us; it strives not to defeat another will but, rather, endeavors to battle *together* in order to fight for the truth and the blessings that truth has for us. With intimacy, ultimate victory is learning what's right and then living it together.

Like the more accurate understanding of commitment we described, goodwill is best understood in terms of active participation as a force of good and wise intent. It's proactive, alive, dynamic. Goodwill is not a passive virtue.

The Bible underscores the importance of wisdom in the creation of goodwill. God "gave Joseph wisdom and enabled him to gain the goodwill of Pharaoh king of Egypt; so [Pharaoh] made him ruler over Egypt and all his palace" (Acts 7:10). Wisdom did double duty: It blessed the Egyptian government with increased insight, and the harmoniousness it fostered ushered in a spirit of cooperation.

Wise counsel blesses others with discernment and insight into their problems. The person receiving this gift feels warm regard for the one who provides such counsel, who in turn is blessed emotionally and spiritually when the wisdom is heeded. This continues to build and strengthen the will to do good.

How Do You Know If You Have It?

Again, the will to do good toward your CNG is more than having good feelings for him (thank goodness). Though good feelings are important, goodwill must also include kindness, consideration, thoughtfulness, and practical support. This is wonderful news for CNG wives, because controlling how we feel is often harder than exerting our will to determine our good actions.

It's okay and even normal to have mixed feelings about him at times. Nothing about that disqualifies you. You can have both good and bad feelings and still produce actions of goodwill.

> **YOU CAN HAVE BOTH GOOD AND BAD FEELINGS AND STILL PRODUCE ACTIONS OF GOODWILL.**

Mixed feelings, though, may cause you to wonder if you possess goodwill toward him at all. Here's a "goodwill thinking" checkup for clarification on this.

When I think of my partner, my thoughts are generally positive.
☐ Most of the time ☐ Sometimes ☐ Not often

I feel proud of my partner.
☐ Most of the time ☐ Sometimes ☐ Not often

I take my partner's feelings and wants into consideration.
☐ Most of the time ☐ Sometimes ☐ Not often

I look forward to seeing my partner at the end of the day.
☐ Most of the time ☐ Sometimes ☐ Not often

I feel our relationship is fair.
☐ Most of the time ☐ Sometimes ☐ Not often

I get the kind of support I need from my partner.
☐ Most of the time ☐ Sometimes ☐ Not often

My partner seems genuinely interested in how my day went.

☐ Most of the time ☐ Sometimes ☐ Not often

We have fun together.
☐ Most of the time ☐ Sometimes ☐ Not often

I feel blessed that we ended up together.
☐ Most of the time ☐ Sometimes ☐ Not often

If it was important for my partner to change careers, I'd find a way to be supportive.
☐ Very likely ☐ Maybe ☐ Probably not

If I had it to do over, I'd still want to be with my partner.
☐ Very likely ☐ Maybe ☐ Probably not

I can easily recall many wonderful moments we've shared.
☐ Very likely ☐ Maybe ☐ Probably not

For each "Most of the time" or "Very probably," give yourself two points.

For each "Sometimes" or "Maybe," give yourself one point.

For each "Not often" or "Probably not," give yourself zero points.

Where you stand:

21–24 Goodwill is present and rather strong.
18–20 Goodwill is moderate.
15–17 Goodwill is present but modest.
12–14 Goodwill is shaky.
 9–11 Ill will is often present.
  6–8 Ill will is almost as strong as goodwill.
  0–5 Goodwill is almost absent.[1]

For some, this self-exam brings a sigh of relief. For others, a sigh of pain. If you feel that hope is something only others experience, know that Sandy's goodwill score once wasn't nearly as strong as it is today. The condition of your tired and wounded heart doesn't have to be fatal or debilitating.

We'll show you ways to improve your goodwill. And goodwill often perpetuates growth: the more you feel it, the more you want to give it. Your marital frustrations won't appear so large and bothersome, and the CNG frustrations will appear more manageable as well.

What Low Goodwill Looks Like

Actions that go hand-in-hand with low levels of goodwill and with the presence of ill will are harsh, hostile, and controlling. Hyper-spiritualism, described earlier, often intensifies the effects of these destructive elements. In sharp contrast, as believers we are to reflect and exude God's amazing grace. Our love and our goodwill are to be lived and shared in response to the wondrous gift of life we have received from "the God and Father of our Lord Jesus Christ, the Father of mercies and the God of all comfort, who comforts us in all our affliction" (2 Corinthians 1:3–4 NASB).

Goodwill, present in most marriages when vows were exchanged, can become virtually buried under the rubble of anger, resentment, and dwindling respect (see chapter 7). Coming to terms with these emotions is vital if you're going to give your efforts to helping intimacy grow.

There are women who no longer possess functioning goodwill. If this describes you, I would advise your husband *not* to open his heart and mind to you—doing so would be extremely dangerous. That vulnerability would damage him even more; you are almost certain to mishandle and disparage his timid emotions, just as he would be encouraging your sins to root deeper and continue their spread. Your children would also likely witness searing and foul behavior that would poison their view of marriage. If you lack goodwill, you need to take up the task of becoming a worthy steward of your husband's heart.

Two CNG marriages come to mind as I write about deficient good-will. Neither husband garnered much natural respect by how he lived and carried himself. Neither performed at home like his wife wanted. Neither consistently exemplified the tougher virtues.

Neither wife felt well taken care of, protected, or cherished. At the same time, both wives seemed to have a slogan written on their fore-heads: "Life should be done *my* way. *I* know best." When one husband, a pastor, acted in any way his wife deemed unpleasant, she would tell him he wasn't behaving as a Christian man should and that he should "get back on the cross," hyper-spiritual talk meaning that he was to always sacrifice for her wants and needs. He wasn't allowed to have flaws, much less his own normal wants and needs.

When the other husband wanted to move his family to take a job that provided better for them, she refused—she would not consider being apart from her family of origin. Neither wife trusted her husband and thereby continually diminished their goodwill. Both undercut their CNGs in front of friends and family, and, horrifically, both actively tried to turn their children against their fathers.

Both of these couples divorced.

These two examples must be put into context. CNG marriages don't always go bad because one partner is rigid and uncooperative. Good-will, a practical manifestation of grace, gets depleted when men are untrustworthy and fail to be assertive in the care of their families. The poor choices a man makes are no one else's responsibility.

That said, it's often true that wives who don't possess goodwill have an ongoing, driving need to be right. With their words and their actions, they claim that what's wrong with the world is everybody else.

Most of us have this tendency, but for some people it's practically a career. The truth is, *Marriage is a privilege, as well as a right.* If what a wife really wants is to win arguments and to make her guy pay full-price for his transgressions, she not only needs to think about why she even wants to be married but also, and more significantly, she needs to begin thinking about how life now and life eternally would be if God took the same approach with her. If it's debate victory she desires, better that she become an attorney and pick her own cases. She's likely to be happier and less frustrated. And he certainly will be.

Being Number One

Cecil G. Osborne, author of *The Art of Understanding Your Mate*, gives excellent insight into a CNG wife:

> [Constance,] a delightful and intelligent divorced woman with three marriages behind her, joined a group, bringing with her a man whom she contemplated marrying. It developed that her three previous husbands had all been alcoholics. When she married them there was no evidence of alcoholism, but as tensions mounted, each became a problem drinker. She took one of the personality inventories with the group and was horrified to discover that she scored ninety-one on dominance. She was also quite high on aggression. Outwardly feminine, *she was unaware of these traits within herself* [emphasis added].
>
> She began to discover why she had married three men who became alcoholics. Problem drinkers are virtually all passive, dependent individuals. Some who have a capacity for hostility could be labeled passive-aggressive individuals. Because of her innate need to control, she had unconsciously chosen passive men; they, being passive and dependent, had unconsciously sought her strength, which they lacked in themselves. Consciously she wanted a strong, gentle husband. Unconsciously she was seeking one who would be weak enough so that she could control him, and consequently each marriage ended in disaster. . . .

Constance had experienced twenty years of marital uproar before she finally sought a divorce. In counseling sessions I came to discover that I was dealing with two women, in a sense, instead of one. Initially she displayed a quiet, passive, martyr-like personality. She manifested this "self" for months, during which time she was separated from her husband. When her husband returned and they made a new start, the passive, gentle personality began to disappear. In its place I began to discover a strong, intractable, unyielding, dominant personality. . . . Her marriage ended in divorce.[2]

> **GOING FOR NUMBER ONE IS GREAT IF YOU WANT TO BRING HOME OLYMPIC GOLD, BUT IT'S DISASTROUS IF YOU WANT TO REMAIN MARRIED.**

Going for number one is great if you want to bring home Olympic gold, but it's disastrous if you want to remain married. Note again the statement (above) that we emphasized in italics: Constance was unaware of those traits within herself. If you've been on planet Earth long enough, you know we sometimes behave in ways that we just don't see. We need others to help us with our blind spots. Go to someone you trust, someone you know to be honest even when her honesty may sting. Ask her if she thinks you have any of the colors of Constance in you; breathe deeply, and really listen to her answer.

Also, ask your husband if, in any way, shape, or form, he feels you try to direct his answers or punish him if he responds in ways you don't like. Intimacy is created through the Third Path of Us, not the One Path of Me.

A Goodwill Exercise

Here is an exercise to help you grow goodwill toward your CNG. As a favor to yourself, do it in a quiet place and during an uninterrupted time. It may be hard with children around; perhaps awaken earlier than usual, when the house is quiet.

> Imagine your CNG as a child going through tough times.
> Imagine him lonely now.
> Imagine him old and disabled.
> Think about his good qualities.
> Recall how you fell in love.
> Think about what you would miss about him if he died.[3]

Consider journaling your answers. If you're new to journaling, you're in for a blessing. Writing down what you think and feel about your marriage can be like peeling an orange, then savoring its aroma and taste. You can journal about a relational aspect for just fifteen minutes and find yourself blessed by insights you wouldn't have imagined when you first began. Journaling was a favored activity of none less than the apostle Paul, who wrote to young Timothy, "When you come, bring the cloak I left with Carpus at Troas, and the books, above all my notebooks" (2 Timothy 4:13 TLB).

Forget Chemistry

Foster goodwill and you foster compatibility, which is *not* the result of two sets of personal traits that magically and effortlessly fit together. Like goodwill, it's what you make, rather than what you already are. Compatibility, writes Hara Estroff Marano, is "a process, one that you negotiate as you go along. Again and again. It's a disposition, an attitude, a willingness to work."[4]

According to contemporary views of compatibility, or what's also called chemistry, *we* should really be divorced. We're both the babies of our families of origin, so we're both supposed to want life our way. We should be less reliable and spoiled. The aggressive-passive nature of our early marriage, if we listened to the culture's lockstep view of "chemistry," should have told us we "just weren't meant for each other." We should have chalked one up to experience and moved on.

What was the initial result of our mixture of traits? We blamed, shamed, and attacked each other, and that unholy trinity of marital strife was made worse when we each tried to drag God to our side. At times we showed about as much goodwill as a hemorrhoid-stricken cattle herder.

But something came and saved us: a willingness to try something different, a manifestation of humility. We tried, mistakes and all, to get out from under our own point of view and at least attempt to hear what the other person was saying. We didn't know where it would lead us. We groped along, stumbled, and somehow were able to avoid completely falling down. We think that God helped us because he shows grace to the humble.

Acts of goodwill—treating each other well even when we didn't feel like it—*not* the wishful thinking of chemistry, came through for us. The will to do good, even when our hearts weren't exactly in it and we didn't know exactly what to do, got us more than through the hard times. It created better times. It was the difference between trying to stay married and wanting to be married.

When it comes to love and intimacy, goodwill is like silverware; almost everyone can learn how to use it, even though we weren't born already knowing how, and even though some of us took a long time to try it and become accustomed to it. Goodwill is remarkably practical and beneficial for those who produce it and receive it.

And, thank God, it's more than a feeling. It's a dynamic force, a tangible action that nurtures intimacy. When married to wisdom, goodwill is bolstered by a forward-moving intent to create goodness and steer clear of evil.

Whether or not your goodwill is lower than you know is good for your marriage, consider even more practical ways to ignite intimacy, found in the next chapter.

CHAPTER 9

MORE PRACTICAL WAYS TO NURTURE INTIMACY

God gave me a unique perspective and worthy dreams.
God gave me words of influence to use for good. But I
didn't use them. I didn't show up. I might have been there
physically, but my gifts—my soul—didn't show up. I didn't
value what I had to offer enough to actually offer it.[1]

LYNNE HYBELS

You may have discerned by now that you have a low level of the *will to do good* when it comes to your CNG. Or you may have found that goodwill is present but that intimacy is not as present as you want. Either way, this chapter is for you. Here's more practical advice on how to build both goodwill and your worthy dream of intimacy.

Express Yourself, Then Listen With Empathy

One study shows that the average married couple actively communicates just twenty-seven minutes a week! Most every business would crash and burn under the same priorities and circumstances.

This reinforces what we've repeatedly stated: Our intimacy-unfriendly culture frequently hinders close emotional attachment. Self-expression and mutual expression are lacking in *most* marriages. Here's how to hone your wise-as-a-serpent skills in this area.

Expressing yourself in a truthful, concise, non-shaming, and gracious manner builds intimacy. Conversely, many of us expect our spouse to somehow read our hearts and minds to discover how we feel and think. I have said numerous times to Sandy, half-joking, half-serious, that she must forgive me for not yet knowing or understanding because I flunked clairvoyance in college.

However, expressing yourself well is only half the undertaking. Listening with empathy is also foundational, especially since most of us have not experienced (regularly or ever) true empathetic listening. Most of us know of and have been highly exposed to passive and selective listening that focuses or tunes in on what relates to us.

Empathetic listening includes two crucial elements: undivided attention, and feeling what your partner feels. Feeling what he feels is particularly beneficial, for while he has feelings, sometimes he has great difficulty labeling and processing them. You can be a huge help to him!

Adults who had troubled childhoods, says Lori Gordon, possess an "emotional allergy."[2] Emotional discomfort and pain in the present remind a CNG of discomfort and pain he experienced as a boy or as a teen, which sets off an emotional reaction that can be intense, irrational, and bewildering. This reaction usually goes in one of two directions: intense withdrawal, or intense counterattack. We don't have to tell you that your guy is far more likely to default toward the former; when he does, you can help him begin to see that painful emotions aren't something to be ashamed about or hide from. You can be instrumental in helping him to vitalize by paying close attention to the tension in his voice and the expression on his face. Then share with him, empathetically, what you have witnessed. For example, simply telling him that he looks sad can bring significant revelation and relief to him.

Most people tend to react to truthful and uncomfortable conversations in one of four ways: they placate, they blame, they detach (remain unemotional), or they redirect. Though CNGs are capable of all four, they tend to placate and remain unemotional. Here's how to reach yours in conversation.

EMPATHETIC LISTENING INCLUDES TWO CRUCIAL ELEMENTS: UNDIVIDED ATTENTION, AND FEELING WHAT YOUR PARTNER FEELS.

The placater is a people-pleasing peace-faker. Female placaters tend to be unable to say no to relational requests. Male placaters, says John Townsend, tend to have a hard time saying no to tasks. "They might lend their lawn mower to a neighbor even though they don't like him, or they'll say yes to extra responsibilities at work." Or they might be the one to always help their overly demanding parents, even giving their own wife and children short shrift. That's particularly unhealthy "because a clear marker of adulthood is that you leave your family of origin, and the family you create has to come first."[3]

Guys who appease and placate say everything's okay when it's not. Getting walked on makes them feel worthless, but they justify their self-made suffering by saying they're suffering for their faith, which is rarely true. They hold in all forms of anger, thinking all anger is sinful, and statistically they're prone to depression and illness. To reach this kind of CNG, let him know he *can* express anger (though not destructive rage). The free expression of anger is a testament to the strength, not the weakness, of your relationship.

The placating CNG lives in fear of losing relationships, of hurting other people, and of receiving another's anger. Assure him by letting him know he will not lose you if he's truthful with you. At other times, seek to express your own anger without being unfair or abusive.

The CNG who remains unemotional is so "reasonable" that he doesn't even seem human. If he's angry, he pretends he's not. "Upset? Who's upset? I'm not upset. I don't get upset." Fear of his emotions makes him want others to stay clear of their feelings too.

Ask him how he's feeling, and if he persistently pretends he's not feeling anything negative, tell him in a respectful way how you disagree. Remind him that the Gospels (especially Mark) show Jesus as more emotional (not less) than those around him. Help him to see in his heart and his mind that expressing emotion is not wrong.

Logic works best when it's connected to emotion. Being analytical and rational all the time isn't enough to live well. Love possesses no physical weight; intimacy, no physical breadth, yet our lives atrophy without them. As someone who has spent most of his life in his head, I (Paul) know just how damaging this approach is to others. It's cruel because it inevitably discredits their feelings and intuitions and ideas. It robs them of identity and value.

If a man's child comes to him crying, and if he tells her "there's nothing to be upset about," how is she being valued and considered? If she has experienced nothing to be upset about, why is she upset? Does telling her she's being illogical for having emotions make any sense?

Such a man is really saying that his daughter's emotional expression is unjustified and unacceptable; he's "rationally" telling her that her emotions are irrational. He's uncomfortable with emotions, and his own emotional development is stunted, so he's trying to get her to put her feelings in her mind, to place them in a realm where he's more at ease in handling them.

Help Him Understand His Four-Letter Word

There's a four-letter word that haunts CNGs, and they need assistance getting over it. Their driving need to have everything in their world be "fair" takes them out of the game of life, like with this CNG (as told by his ex-girlfriend):

> I picked up *No More Christian Nice Guy* after a breakup with my boyfriend, who fits your description of the CNG. He is thirty-four (I am the first girlfriend he's dated longer than six months) and seems to always be discontent with life and all its hardships. When we were dating, I tried to help him understand that conflict and trials are just part of life, that there are smart ways of dealing with them. But he never appreciated my advice and said I wasn't being empathetic.
>
> It's hard to be empathetic when I feel like the problems in his life are brought upon himself. He broke up with me (despite that he cares and cherishes me) because he thought that our personalities were incompatible, when really I think he can't be compatible with anyone unless he gets rid of the notion that a relationship with the least amount of friction is the right one. Life comes with certain obstacles, and facing them is healthy, and it's something he doesn't understand.

Obsessing over what's fair and what's ideal is a hallmark CNG error, made worse by his thinking that if he adheres to all the right rules, then life will reward him with a carefree existence. This flies in the face of Scripture and experience. Sometimes behaving virtuously will get you in trouble; Jesus says, "You *will* have trouble in this world. But take heart! I have overcome the world" (John 16:33, emphasis added).

There exists in this realm an enemy of our soul, Satan, the father of lies (8:44). The devil doesn't play fair, and he uses the CNG's demand for fairness (already subjective, and often faulty) to steal his life from him.

Meditate on Ecclesiastes 8:14, then share your insight with your CNG:

> Here's something that happens all the time and makes no sense at all: Good people get what's coming to the wicked, and bad people get what's coming to the good. I tell you, this makes no sense. It's smoke. (THE MESSAGE)

Also, heed these words from Madame Jeanne Guyon:

> If knowing the answers to life's questions is absolutely necessary to you, then forget the journey. You will never make it, for this is a journey of unknowables . . . and most of all, things unfair.[4]

Unfairness is sometimes the way of the world. God has never promised us immediate fairness; he guarantees ultimate justice. Help your CNG to see and embrace this by showing him how you won't let unfairness stop you from being proactive. Show him, through your life, how to chart a new life-path. Help him understand that one of the best ways to take the sting out of life's unfairness is to set reasonable goals that can be obtained with time and effort.

GOD HAS NEVER PROMISED US IMMEDIATE FAIRNESS; HE GUARANTEES ULTIMATE JUSTICE.

Instead of complaining about others, focus on your growth, healing, and development. Instead of praying to be delivered from life's inevitable difficulties, pray for strength to endure, and let him see your struggles, warts and all. Seeing this may well help him stop the unnecessary bleeding of energy that flows from complaining about how unfair life is. Joyful, hopeful people know the world is not always fair; they charge ahead anyway.

Model Optimism

Optimism is another area where you can help your CNG become more intimate with you. Behind his deceptive smile is the belief that most everyone and everything is out to get him. He doesn't really believe in God's grace; he's trying to please God with nice behavior. He doesn't believe God loves him and has good plans for him. He thinks he's gaining brownie points solely through his works, and he's not exercising faith. His fearful disposition has him playing defense, robbing him of closeness and connection. Optimism is hope's first cousin; your CNG needs to know how important optimism is for both of you.

To elevate optimism, meditate on hope-filled biblical passages, with one important stipulation. Two extreme and unfruitful approaches to biblical truth are either making it say more than it really says or ignoring/downplaying its counsel and applicability. One fearful CNG approach is memorizing enough verses and praying the right prayer(s) to "make it all go away." As Chuck Swindoll cautions, "Overcoming those anxious fears won't be as easy as simply sitting in a church service or finding some magical Bible verse."[5]

Applied rightly, the Bible is immensely helpful in dealing with fear's debilitating effects. The influential pragmatist William James credited the Bible for holding him together.

> The fear [in my life] was so invasive and powerful that if I had not clung to scripture-texts like "The eternal God is my refuge," etc. "come unto me, all ye that labor and are heavy-laden," etc. I think I should have grown really insane.[6]

One excellent passage for meditation is Jeremiah 29:11–12:

> I alone know my purpose for you, says the Lord: prosperity and not misfortune, and a long line of children after you. If you invoke me and pray to me, I will listen to you. (NEB)

Include this in your own regular reading and prayers. Pull out that journal and write down what these words mean in your life; share your good news with your husband. Seek to help him understand that God is in his corner.

There's growing evidence that this very change in thinking is one of the best ways to ward off depression and related maladies like listlessness, which leads to directionless living. Harvard graduates who were most pessimistic in 1946 were also the least healthy when restudied in 1980. Virginia Tech students who were pessimistic suffered more colds, sore throats, and flues. Optimistic people suffer less illness and recover better from cancer and surgery.

Nevertheless, perspective and balance are important. Unchecked optimism, much like hyper-spiritualism, can spell frustration; optimism isn't choosing to believe that something isn't what it is. In order to be wise as a serpent, follow this recipe: for newfound hope, mix in all the optimism that comes your way, then add shrewdness, as exemplified in the life of Jesus. Honesty and common sense both check optimism from becoming a tendency to create false realities.

> **OPTIMISM ISN'T CHOOSING TO BELIEVE THAT SOMETHING ISN'T WHAT IT IS.**

Optimism, properly applied, shows that setbacks are not fatal and are often opportunities for embarking on a new path. A person who confronts life with a yes-attitude is more adventurous and attractive and has a greater capacity for intimacy.

Find Grace

If you attend a fear-based church that dwells heavily on legalism and condemnation, your issues associated with hopelessness and lack of optimism will be extenuated and intensified. It's essential that CNGs experience God's amazing grace.

There's a phenomenon that haunts CNGs who had abusive or neglect-filled childhoods: They are drawn toward and vulnerable to abusive individuals and groups. Nowhere is this more insidious than in church. Where you attend and invest is of great import; be willing to change, if necessary, if doing so means his transformation can be successful. Specifically, *people with troubled pasts that facilitate passivity should avoid churches that make them feel ashamed for being human.*

There are churches that don't treat people this way. The grace you receive there may feel strange and even wrong at first—it did for us—but please, persevere. Here's a checklist of what to look for regarding spiritual abuse. Like popular Christian writer Philip Yancey had to do, if you've experienced it and been wounded by it, you will need to undertake forgiveness toward an institution that has perpetuated or endorsed it, just as you would need to forgive abusive or neglectful parents.

- ◉ Does your church/pastor often denounce other churches for not being truly "Christian"?
- ◉ Are criticisms about your church characterized by your church as "attacks from Satan/the enemy"?
- ◉ Does your church have leaders who portray themselves as spiritually and morally superior because they are part of "God's anointed"?
- ◉ Does your church pressure people to attend all church functions?
- ◉ Do your church's leaders claim to have special insight into Scripture that others don't possess—and that, therefore, their actions shouldn't be questioned?
- ◉ Does your church manipulate people through intimidation and shame?
- ◉ Do you feel worthless and deprived of human dignity after sermons?
- ◉ Do people drop other activities (school) and responsibilities (commitment to spouse and children) in order to be at church and "work for the Lord"?
- ◉ Would leaving your church be accompanied by warnings of divine

judgment and withheld "blessings" from leadership?

◗ Has someone you trust and respect warned you about your church?

Model Assertiveness

Another practical way you can help your husband break out from the CNG lifestyle and into the world of emotional engagement is to model assertiveness. Assertive people state their feelings and thoughts and exert their will while still being respectful of others. Aggressive people attack or ignore other people's feelings, thoughts, and will. Passive people . . . well, we don't have to tell you.

Here's a quick list of how these three types behave in the same situation. Refer to it regularly if being assertive is difficult for you also.

	Passive:	*Aggressive:*	*Assertive:*
In a Group:	Afraid to speak up. Isolates.	Interrupts and talks over others. Controls.	Speaks openly. Doesn't try to control what others think, feel, and do.
Quality of Voice:	Speaks softly.	Speaks loudly.	Uses a conversational tone that doesn't whimper or demand.
State of Eyes:	Avoids eye contact.	Glares.	Makes solid eye contact.
Facial Expressions:	Shows little or no expression.	Intimidates.	Expressions match the message.

Body Posture:	Slouches and withdraws.	Stands rigidly, crosses arms, leans into another's space.	Relaxes, shows open posture and expressions.
Handling Feelings:	Dishonest. Pretends to agree with others at all times.	Considers only own feelings.	Honest.
Treating Hurts:	Hurts self to avoid hurting others.	Hurts others before they can cause hurt.	Tries to avoid hurting others and self.
Handling Goals:	Doesn't reach them. May not have any.	Hurts others while reaching them.	Endeavors to reach goals without hurting others.
View of Self:	You're okay. I'm not.	I'm okay. You're not.	We're both sinners in need of God's grace. I respect you even when I disagree with your behavior.

Modeling assertiveness will help your CNG be able to see what he's missing by being so passive. He'll see that he has real choices that influence the quality of his life based upon how he presents himself and treats others.

Share Your Power in the Home

I grew up in a home with one Official Mood: Mother's. The unstated Coughlin Family Motto: *Mom feels this way, so it's true.* She could rarely be swayed, even when presented with solid arguments to the contrary. The family lived under the tyranny of feelings, whether or not they were just or right.

No one, usually, was allowed to have an opinion or emotions that differed much from what she was thinking or feeling at the time. This was an abuse of power, especially to the men, who were expected to do their part and then remain basically silent; she didn't like "male energy." Book critic Natalie Jost remembers a similar dynamic in her home:

> I had a great time reading [*No More Christian Nice Guy*], thanking God all the way through it, for giving Paul this wisdom. . . . I grew up in a home where women ruled the roost. Men were to love and work, then come home and be quiet. Any time my father or stepfather, uncle or grandfather, tried to speak up about an issue, they were quickly hushed by a scolding look from their spouse.

Jost had a brother, raised only by her mother, who was encouraged not to defend himself and to bury his anger and frustrations. "One day he snapped and landed himself in jail at the young age of fifteen. He's almost thirty now and hasn't seen much daylight since his teens."

Such a home not only helps create anxious and fearful Nice Guys, it also makes it far less likely that they'll break out of their passive confines. It's essential that CNG wives share domestic power justly.

- Allow him to have a say in how your home is decorated. Ask him what style he likes. Many men prefer clean visual lines in their homes—it puts their minds at ease. Most don't like knickknacks; if yours doesn't, consider reducing their general presence by a third. Don't assume he wants everything covered with lace or pillows; give him a voice, and let a masculine spirit share in your home's look and feel.
- If he does home repairs, treat them as acts of love, perhaps like meal preparation is considered.

- If you control the social calendar, start adding his friends and family to it, if they aren't on the list already. Many men say they don't see their friends much after marriage. This isn't always coincidental. If your husband limited your contact with your friends and family, how would you feel?

- Nurture robust debate and opinion-sharing.

- Let him get a dog if he wants one. (Our vote: a cairn terrier!)

- Encourage roughhousing with the kids, and don't monitor it. Expect minor bumps and scrapes. Most kids love roughhousing with their dad. *Note:* The worst that usually happens is a scratch. (Dads, trim your fingernails.)

- Let kids get messy. Tip: Invest in a utility sink.

- If he doesn't load the dishwasher "right," it might be best to keep this to yourself.

- Let family members express anger, helping them channel it into healthy action.

- If he likes to watch sports, slow down enough to enjoy at least one game a week. We know a woman's work is never done, but this may be a realistic sacrifice that helps your campaign for intimacy.

Your home could be a launching pad for change, a theater of transformation where you can fortify his ability to be assertive and in the process greatly increase your chances of intimacy. Helping him feel safe saying no to you around the house will bolster his ability to say no to a persuasive salesman at the door, no to his parents, no to working late when it's not necessary . . . you get the picture.

Make Room for Your Guy in Your Mind

You must make room in your mind for regular, positive thoughts about your CNG. Some you can write about; in your journal, make a list of encouraging thoughts you can ponder on a regular basis. Suggestions:

- ◗ The things that physically attract you to him.
- ◗ Something about him you cherish.
- ◗ The greeting at workday's end that you think he'd like to receive.
- ◗ Cuddling in bed, making love.
- ◗ Giving him his favorite form of affection.
- ◗ Having a meal together without much distraction.
- ◗ Planning a night out together.
- ◗ Something about which you need to be more understanding.
- ◗ Something for which to apologize.[7]

Put these reminders in various places to encourage your consistent positive thinking about him. It will help you appreciate his good side, and he'll feel it.

Get Yourself Under Healthy Control

Once again, it's important that you get your own emotions under control. Sometimes our emotions are more connected to how we feel physically than we realize. Take an inventory of what you eat, how much (or little) you sleep, the quality of your sleep, and what kind of regular exercise you get. I (Sandy) had my hormone levels tested, adjusted them, and felt much better afterward. Both of us have regular exercise programs; at my 5:00 a.m. running group, I get a physical workout *and* forty-five minutes of talking.

Take care of yourself; living with a CNG requires more energy. Give your body what it needs to provide the strength you must have.

Turning a Situational No Into an Overarching Yes

We've written much about the importance of sexual intimacy to most men; wives sometimes have to accept by faith that this is true. Our gender differences make us different; the sooner we accept them, the happier we'll be.

For example, I don't understand why the Coughlin home has to be so neat and tidy. Like most men, I have a higher tolerance for mess. But I've come to realize that for many women, a home is an extension of who they are. An unkempt home feels to a woman like ten extra pounds on her hips. I don't experience that feeling, but I accept it as valid and important.

We urge you to take the same approach toward sexual relations with your husband. Accept his need as good—different, but right. It's not that you don't have sexual needs; it's that his are more predominant.

And don't forget how important respect for him and faith in him are in unlocking his sexual passion. Writes Dr. Coleman:

> Men want respect, which includes the knowledge that you have faith in him. The words "I have faith in you" tap into a man's deep-seated, hard-wired need to provide for and protect the people he loves. It indicates that he is trustworthy and that he can be counted on to do the right thing. . . . And if he is not struggling with any addiction or any severe personality disorder, it will awaken or super-charge his feelings of love and passion. He will crave more intimacy. Of course, he might show it in his most natural way of wanting sex. But it won't be sex for the sake of sex. It will be sex for the sake of you, the woman; sex where he wants to melt into you and never let you go. Sex where he wants to enter your soul.[8]

At the same time, let's be realistic: Sometimes sex just isn't in the cards. Other demands require our attention. It's okay to say no, but it's best to say yes whenever possible. Here are some good ways to break bad news:

- ❍ "I love you so much, but I'm just not in the mood right now. I promise I'll make it up to you!" (Then make good on the promise.)
- ❍ "Would you mind if we just cuddled this time?"
- ❍ "I know it has been a while since we made love, but now isn't the best time for me. Can we set another time?"

Here's what not to say:

- "Is sex all you ever think about?"
- "Can't you see I'm exhausted?"
- "All right, make it quick."

Or you say nothing but flinch roughly when touched.

Making Time for One Another

A stressed-out, so-busy-I-can't-find-my-purse lifestyle often direly lacks intimacy. There's no substitute for time together. If you can't remember the last time you shared hysterical laughter, you are in desperate need of some mutual fun. Some ways to create time for intimacy:

- Say no to low-priority tasks. Some things really can wait.
- Occasionally ask friends or family to assist.
- Make ordinary, mundane projects more fun to do together. Listen to music when working on the yard or around the house. Buy special coffee drinks when doing home improvement projects. (And so on.)
- Turn off the TV and computers.
- Plan a frozen-pizza dinner for the kids, then sneak out to a nearby restaurant for a date. Share entrees to keep down both pounds and cost. Reserve this time for talking about issues that make you feel good together.

Making time for each other doesn't have to be a huge production. Everyday small talk is a great intimacy builder. Some do's and don'ts for making small talk something bigger:

- Do try to sit together, lie down together, or touch during small talk.
- Do limit the conversation to everyday, non-conflict issues.
- Do "informalize" the time by sharing back or foot rubs, taking a walk, cuddling, coffee or tea, music, and so on.

- Do keep competing tasks (cooking, changing clothes, dealing with kids or pets or telephones) at an absolute minimum while chatting.
- Don't get aggravated or be abrupt.
- Don't discuss controversial topics or begin to criticize.
- Don't feel forced to keep the conversation moving; periods of silence are okay if you're connecting physically.[9]

GUY TO GUY

Self-disclosure is a requirement in married intimacy. Without it, you're unknowable, and you seem evasive and robotic. "That's just the way I am" isn't going to cut it; go ahead and say it if you want, but realize it's loser talk. We're not born into a holding pattern; saying we already are who we need and want to be foolishly denies our need for spiritual and emotional growth.

Eventually your wife will go from thinking you're presently unknowable to thinking you'll never be knowable. She may eventually run out of ideas and give up trying. Many men have a hard time revealing who they are, so you have a lot of company. But some of them are down at divorce court; this is serious. The fact is, avoiding self-disclosure makes your life harder, now and later.

Here's a challenge: Over the next eight weeks, reveal eight facts about your life that you're pretty sure your wife doesn't know. Accompany these words with physical affection, even in public. And remember: facts about your life don't equal disclosure about your life. Share how they made or make you feel. Begin to reveal yourself from the inside.

Wives, if you're reading this, when your husband does get to this tremulous point, don't correct or give advice. Ask questions that will help you understand him better. Listen for words that carry emotional power. Let him know how they make you feel, but don't present your feelings in a way that puts him on the defensive.

Please don't tell him that all he has to do is "pray through the problem" or "give it to God" or "consider it all joy." Don't just tell him you're going to pray that he be delivered from what ails him. Yes, he needs to pray and trust God with his pain, but those aren't the only things he should do. Your words can nurture *or* strangle intimacy. You got married to be known by someone and to know someone in a way no other relationship can provide. If you want to know him, listen to him. We get married for intimate companionship, not to be each other's spiritual guide.

Sincerity and Weakness

Mark Twain said he could live weeks off of one sincere compliment. Compliments do wonders for CNGs as well. Praise and approval are key ingredients in the intimacy mix.

Praise your CNG in a way that's sincere and shows humility. To do this, you'll have to be honest with your own weakness. And *honest* doesn't mean making something up or pretending that something's a weakness when it's apparent you don't think so. Saying "I know I can be hard to deal with, sometimes" and not meaning it doesn't work. It just sends mixed signals.

If you sincerely reveal weakness to your CNG, it can do wonders to get him to open up. He already knows you think he has weaknesses; if you admit your own, he will begin to comprehend that you are in the marriage boat together.

Humility goes hand-in-hand with a teachable spirit, in moving away from thinking that your point of view is always the right one. Sandy's move toward being teachable came when she sensed that God had some-thing different in mind for dealing with me (Paul). God helped her put aside preconceived notions and consider the possibility that God might be redirecting her. This flexibility fueled my transformation. Chains began to lift and fall. I spent less time defending myself and more time moving closer to her.

While we're on the subject of compliments: If a basement person puts your man down, never go along with it, especially in public. Do not remain neutral to the attack upon him either. (Remaining neutral is just a tiny bit better than assailing him.) Be a balcony person and come to his defense, which might mean

HUMILITY GOES HAND-IN-HAND WITH A TEACHABLE SPIRIT IN MOVING AWAY FROM THINKING THAT YOUR POINT OF VIEW IS ALWAYS THE RIGHT ONE.

both of you leaving the scene. Also, compliment him in front of friends and family. When possible, compliment what's important to him or something he does well.

When the Table Turns

As we've talked about before, it's a nearly sacred event when a passive person steps up to the plate of life and swings. So if he comes to you with a complaint about you that's not abusive in content (words) or form (e.g., rage), allow him room to make mistakes. Don't pick his words apart. He likely won't handle the event as smoothly as you could. That's all right. Let him be him.

Be smart in your defense of yourself. Don't come out swinging—part of intimacy is feeling comfortable complaining, which will make him more knowable. Really listen to what he has to say, and weigh his words in your mind. Keep your response short, and if you need more time to think about what he said, tell him so. Say "we" whenever possible instead of "you." End with some form of affection.

Spouses who want to rescue their CNGs when they do finally open up tend to want to put out the fire of pain too soon, offering advice and solutions too quickly. Don't try to fix his problems. Do try to help him express them. His pain, frustration, and confusion need to be expressed if he's to become more alive emotionally and closer to you.

Don't Stand in the Way of Professional Help

We once attended a church where the pastor had had an idyllic childhood. He spoke glowingly about how he never heard his father or mother yell. Physical violence was alien, and support was constant. They did a great job of fortifying his young psyche; he was among the most confident people we've ever known.

Sadly, he criticized people who reached out for help with their troubled childhoods and organizations like Focus on the Family that encourage such help. He thought all counseling, including from a Christian perspective, was of the devil, designed to keep us away from leaning solely on Christ. Many listened to him, and in so doing made their lives worse.

He was a man who knew grief as an adult, so he felt qualified to lecture about the entire world of grief. He failed to distinguish that pain as a child is far more fundamental and bewildering than pain as an adult. Anyone in the same misguided camp would do well to consider what C. S. Lewis wrote about receiving professional help in *Mere Christianity*. "Psychoanalysis itself, apart from all the philosophical additions that Freud and others have made to it, is not in the least contradictory to Christianity." Lewis said there are irrational fears "which no amount of moral effort can do anything about" and that "bad psychological material is not a sin but a disease. It does not need to be repented of, but to be cured."[10]

Humans, he wrote, judge one another by external actions, which can be deceivingly simple: "God judges them by their moral choices." So when an emotionally troubled person "who has a pathological horror of cats forces himself to pick up a cat for some good reason, it is quite possible that in God's eyes he has shown more courage than a healthy man."

> Some of us who seem quite nice people may, in fact, have made so little use of a good heredity and a good upbringing that we're really worse than those whom we regard as friends. . . . That is why Christians are told not to judge. We see only the results which a man's choices make out of his raw material. But God does not judge him on the raw material at all, but on what he has done with it. . . .
>
> Upon death, all sorts of nice things which we thought our own, but which were really due to a good digestion, will fall off some of us: all sorts of nasty things which were due to complexes or bad health will fall off others. We shall then, for the first time, see every one as he really was. There will be surprises.[11]

Timid CNGs need real help, and sometimes this means talking to counselors who know much about the causes of fear and anxiety. Please don't stand in the way if this is what he decides to do. Remember that God did not give him his current timid spirit (2 Timothy 1:7); his experiences in this world did. If he needs additional insight into who he is, who God really is, and what this life is really about, a wise and empathetic counselor might provide it.

Likewise, be careful with the opposite mistake: demanding that he goes to a counselor. People forced into counseling, even those who need it most, often don't do well. They don't change because they don't think they need to. If you want him to see a counselor, point out, without condemning, how fear and anxiety are holding him back and causing him to sin. Encourage him to read *No More Christian Nice Guy*. In the core of his being, he may come to embrace the truth in these words of the Roman poet Ovid: "Be patient and tough; some day this pain will be useful to you."

Teaching Without Preaching

Sandy is less afraid of death and the life that follows it than your average person. Having worked in kidney dialysis for about twenty years, she has watched many beloved friends slip out of her life.

Sandy's movement toward, instead of away from, people with serious illness has helped her become amazingly compassionate. Recently, at one of our kids' basketball games, sitting by herself was a friend with cancer. Oxygen tubes. Ill-gray skin. A wool stocking cap thick enough for Mount Everest.

No one was sitting on the cold metal chairs on either side of her—not surprising, as moving toward discomfort isn't what most people do. But Sandy moved toward our friend with more than lack of apprehension. She wanted to sit by her, talk with her, be with her. I (Paul) was so proud.

Up until the writing of this book, I had never told her this. I have watched her for nearly two decades bless others while they're dying, and she has shown me that not only can such actions be done, they can be done well. She has inspired me, without one word, to be a better and braver person.

If you want that guy of yours to be more courageous and alive, be so yourself. And let your actions talk for you.

Conclusion

Like Lynne Hybels, quoted at the beginning of this chapter, you have been given a unique perspective and worthy dreams from God. No one knows your CNG like you, and your desire to be closer to him is right and good. Yet as Hybels laments, she didn't use her unique perspective. She didn't honor her worthy dream. She "didn't show up" and didn't value her ability to effect change.

We've noticed a similar dynamic with CNG wives. They don't detect their power, so they don't use it. Their creative strength is often buried under anger, frustration, bitterness, and resentment. Many who do sense their power misspend it. They show up, but it's sometimes the wrong kind of showing up.

The Third Path of Us is blazed when you take legitimate frustrations and warning signs and choose different actions instead, like the ones suggested above. This better approach means being critical without being a critic. Instead of cursing the darkness of emotional detachment, be brave and create light.

CHAPTER 10

DRAWING CLOSER TO HIM, AND TO *HIM*

If you treat a man as he is, he will stay as he is. But if you
treat him as if he were what he ought to be and could be,
he will become the bigger and better man.

JOHAN WOLFGANG VON GOETHE

In Christianity God is not a static thing—not even a person—but a
dynamic, pulsating activity, a life, almost a kind of drama. Almost,
if you will not think me irreverent, a kind of dance.[1]

C. S. LEWIS

You have learned that the best chance of creating greater intimacy
with your CNG begins with you. Much of this book isn't directly
about him. Sure, we've addressed some of the mystery of his perplexing
lifestyle. But the majority of your redemptive work is found in
approaching the problem of emotional detachment by charting a more

creative and empathetic approach toward him. Contrary to what our culture has told us, he isn't so much a problem to be fixed as a person to be understood and appreciated.

Some of his behavior rattles you because it's sinful and because he often disguises his sin behind a fake smile and false relaxedness. But some also gets under your skin because he doesn't view the world with your feminine sensibility. He rattles you because he's a guy. This makes him different, not wrong.

The benefits of a better approach are numerous. Near the top of the list is the substantial reduction of energy-draining and faith-stealing anxiety, which comes from our inability to know our environment and our inability to orient ourselves to our own existence in the real world. Anxiety's attacks compel us to choose cowardice when we feel lost and powerless.

The message we've given you has also emphasized the immense power you have in the life of your CNG. We again want to encourage you to embrace this power, using it justly to create the Third Path of Us.

This powerful work of nurturing another's injured mind and heart is likely to bring you greater intimacy with God as well. It's exciting to realize that what you've been hoping to create, the change you've been praying will occur, has an even more sacred ramification.

Marriage, wrote Katherine Anne Porter, "is the merciless revealer, the great white searchlight turned on the darkest places of human nature."[2] Very few of us realize this as we pop the question, pick out wedding colors, and draft our guest list. But it's true. Marriage is the crucible in which we realize our darkest nature. We discover things about ourselves we do not like, and we wonder during tough times if there is any hope for improvement.

Kathleen and Thomas Hart say,

Sometimes what is hard to take in the first years of marriage is not what we find out about our partner, but what we find out about ourselves. As one young woman who had been married about a year said, "I always thought of myself as a patient and forgiving person. Then I began to wonder if that was just because I had never before gotten close to anyone. In marriage, when John and I began . . . dealing with differences, I saw how small and unforgiving I could be. I discovered a hardness in me I had never experienced before."[3]

Forgiveness. We're stingy when giving it to others. It's hard to love people so different from us. It's difficult for a passive man to love an assertive woman, and vice versa.

Nonetheless, we are called to love even the unlovely and to serve even those who cannot repay us (see Luke 14). If we let differences get in love's way, we shrink our world and become little self-islands. How boring.

And taken to its logical extreme, loving only those we can relate to and who don't challenge us ensures that we'll never love God much either. He is indescribably different from us—for starters, he's skinless, boneless, eternal, and holy. That doesn't mean we can't and shouldn't love him.

Love is learned, and marriage is the most demanding classroom of love. Loving someone who right now appears so unlovely to you may be a larger display of spiritual brawn and faith than all the money you will ever tithe or verses you will ever memorize.

LOVING ONLY THOSE WE CAN RELATE TO AND WHO DON'T CHALLENGE US ENSURES THAT WE'LL NEVER LOVE GOD MUCH EITHER.

God could have designed a different way to form families. But he chose this often-difficult arrangement, and for a reason: Those who make their way through the confusion and into the Third Path of Us become better people.

The need to confront your inner darkness is not the same anywhere else as it is in marriage. The hell you have faced and experienced *can* grow your soul. You can be more loving, caring, understanding, shrewd, authentic, and honest. You can be less judgmental. You can become a brighter redemptive force of light—even if he doesn't change. Your bigger soul will be more attractive than any implant.

So much of this growth revolves around forgiveness. There exists what some might mistakenly call a selfish side to the act of pardoning someone for wrongdoing. This quality isn't selfish, though—just mutually beneficial. Forgiveness, writes Gary Thomas, "is an act of self-defense, a tourniquet that stops the fatal bleeding of resentment."[4] Henri Nouwen defined forgiveness as "love practiced among people who love poorly."[5]

If you think it's too hard to forgive someone who has done horrible things, you need to think again. You can love the sinner and at the same time hate the sin. Wrote C. S. Lewis:

> It occurred to me that there was one man to whom I had been doing this all my life—namely myself. However much I might dislike my own cowardice or conceit or greed, I went on loving myself. There had never been the slightest difficulty about it. In fact the reason why I hated the things was that I loved the man. Just because I loved myself, I was sorry to find that I was the sort of man who did those things.[6]

You have extended such forgiveness over and over to yourself. Consider him as well; stronger ability to forgive will help you do what Francis de Sales advised, to "have contempt for contempt." Have contempt for the belief that your CNG (or anyone, for that matter) is undeserving of your respect. As you know, intimacy cannot grow in the presence of contempt and disrespect.

Criticize by Creating, Not by Being His Critic

The legal state of marriage no more makes you intimate and loving than taking a ferry from one island to another makes you a sailor. Physical proximity is not the issue.

Marriage, like God, is an innately creative entity, which is why rigidity in attitude is among the most prominent intimacy killers. There must be a general, shared life-philosophy for any marriage to flourish and for intimacy to be created and maintained.

Philosophy, a way of explaining basic concepts about life such as truth, cause and effect, and freedom, is innately critical. Philosophy culls, eliminates, and rejects false answers. This often demands that old ways come tumbling down; Picasso said, "Every act of creation is first of all an act of destruction." To the junk heap: your old way of viewing your CNG and your old way of trying to reach him.

This doesn't mean you go around pretending his passive ways are good and helpful— they aren't. It means that as you keep your critical faculties alive and functioning, you do some-

BE CRITICAL BY BECOMING MORE CREATIVE—NOT BEING A CRITIC.

thing different with the information they bring you.

Be critical by becoming more creative—not being a critic in his life. We, being made in God's image, have within us certain characteristics of God that we sometimes forget we possess. Allender and Longman say it this way:

> [We were] meant to be a bold creative artist who plunges into the unformed mystery of life and shapes it to a greater vision of beauty. At the Fall [we] became a cowardly, violent protector of nothing more than [ourselves]. Intimacy and openness were replaced by hiding and hatred.[7]

The Benefits Extend to Children

Not only will these new skills help you forge emotional intimacy in your marriage—thereby fortifying against divorce, increasing your health, and bringing God more glory—you will also learn how to become a better mother by not creating passive Nice Guys and Gals in the first place.

You may find yourself doing what this couple is doing. Here's what they wrote to *Today's Christian Woman* after reading our testimony there:

> The article "No More Christian Nice Guy" affirmed a decision my husband and I made last year. Having a newborn, I began to spend more time with other mothers. I noticed a common phrase to redirect their children was, "Now, honey, that's not nice." I told my husband that I didn't like those words because it teaches a child that the goal is to be "nice." We both agreed that there are times when we need to do what is "right" and not what is "nice." In his article, Coughlin provided examples of when Jesus did the right thing even when others certainly didn't think he was being nice. We have chosen to say to our toddler, "That's not right." Of course, he doesn't understand us yet, but when he does, we want him to learn to always do what is right even if it is not nice.

You Are Never Without Hope

As we said earlier, according to the relationship experts, we should have never gotten married. And we sure shouldn't be happily married.

If Paul had married a different kind of woman, he most likely would not have come to terms with his fear and passivity—he wouldn't have had the motivation to change. If he had married a passive woman, they could have passively floated through life together in a boat with a stubby little rudder. It's good that he married an assertive woman.

And it's good for Sandy to have married someone who, after

acknowledging and facing passivity's badness, retained the benefits of a gracious personality. It helped her become more compassionate and understanding, seasoning her assertive nature just as being more truthful seasoned Paul's graciousness.

What appeared to be a cruel joke of fate turned out to be a soul-expanding experience. We had to push past many of the thoughts and feelings expressed in this letter from a careworn CNG wife:

> I just came across your site after reading the article in *Today's Christian Woman* and thought . . . *Thank God, I'm not crazy.* I've been married for almost five years to my sweetheart who at one point in my life was my hero. His laugh and laid-back personality attracted me to him at first since I'm a more assertive and goal-oriented career woman. But five years later I find myself separated and contemplating divorce.
>
> I've spent endless nights crying over what I've come to see as my "nice" husband who everyone loves but [who] I can't stand anymore. He got suckered by false collection bills and progressed to being suckered by TV and radio scams. He didn't finish his college degree, this after changing degrees three times due to his indecision. We've had age-old conversations about purpose in life and making lifelong goals and how to achieve them, but they fell on deaf ears. He didn't believe in setting goals because "goals set you up for failure."
>
> Then things escalated when he started working for crooks for bosses and not confronting them. I almost came to the point where I thought I was crazy because everyone loved my husband and he is commonly labeled as "perfect." That's not a joke. I hear it from my friends and his family. So you can imagine how he responded to my insight that he had problems with assertiveness, purpose, ambition, accountability, and weak relationships. In eight years of our relationship he has fostered maybe one friendship, and it's a weak one at that.

Other men have confronted him regarding his passivity. Then I get to deal with his rage after the door to our home is shut. He's actually prideful about his passivity. I don't know at this point what will happen in this marriage but your site has given me hope that I'm not alone. I long for my husband to be the man that I really know that he is!!! Thank you for breaking a mold and changing the lives of those around you. I plan on passing this information onto my husband ... maybe he will read it. I would appreciate any prayer.

The following two letters from other couples speak of their journey in progress. This one is from a pastor's wife:

Jeff is doing much better. He's no longer physically ill (was struggling with an esophageal ulcer, migraines, and digestive issues). He went to our church board and shared some things that were going on in the office (probably for years), much to their shock and surprise. Apparently, nobody has ever shared much of the ugliness that happens there. Most of the other pastors are really CNGs "looking out for the team." Sadly, the worst CNG is our lead pastor, who is getting walked on by everyone, I mean *everyone,* and he expected my husband to follow suit.

The long and short of it is that my husband shared in love what was the truth for him. Breaking the CNG code of silence was a big deal for him. He was very scared, and some on the board said nothing. Others commended him for bravely coming forward and said they were impressed with his honesty.

He ended up resigning and was replaced about a week later! Amazing but true. I asked him to respond to your question about the latest in his recovery. He said he never wants to work for a church again. That's really where he is now. We are living off severance and he's looking for other work. God in His Providence has seen to it that we are not in dire straits and I am amazed at His generosity and careful and timely gifts.

Jeff is healthy for the first time in over a year. Strangely, the people looking out for us most now is our congregation. They were so sad to see him go but knew from being longtime members just what he was dealing with. They have given us money, are inviting us to dinner, and are generally praying for God's will in our lives.

Brad and I have gone through some tough times. That's for sure. But we're making progress. I have given him more room like you said and I have tried to be less critical of him. I make mistakes but I'm getting better, and I can tell that he's more comfortable around me now. He is stronger than he used to be.

His job is still tough for him, but he has stood up for himself more than he did before and he feels better about himself. He says he doesn't get picked on as much as he used to.

Now that I have gotten behind him more and I'm better to him, I can see how damaging all my complaining and pushing was to him and us as a family. Everyone is a lot happier. Thank you.

Their inspiration and the information they received on living it out spurred these women to get behind their husbands and go through life together. They are now walking, sometimes stumbling, hand-in-hand together. These women of character possess the kind of strength that helps them to refuse to be either a rolling pin or a doormat.

We don't know all the reasons Jeff and Brad have been doing so well. But we do know one vital power behind their transformation: Both have a woman of goodwill in their corner. When each woman mustered her courage, creativity, and faith, and when each began to rightly trust and use her feminine power and intuition to help forge a third path toward intimacy, her man began to see how intimacy is what they both want and that they're building it. They have discovered that while it's challenging, it's not complicated, this shared life of being both married _and_ engaged.

ENDNOTES

Chapter 1

1. Scott Wetzler, *Living With the Passive-Aggressive Man: Coping With Hidden Aggression—From the Bedroom to the Boardroom* (Wichita, KS: Fireside, 1993), 22.
2. Paul Coleman, *The Complete Idiot's Guide to Intimacy* (New York: Alpha, 2005).
3. Dan Allender and Tremper Longman III, *The Intimate Mystery: Creating Strength and Beauty in Your Marriage* (Downers Grove, IL: InterVarsity Press, 2005).

Chapter 2

1. George Orwell, "Inside the Whale," *Inside the Whale and Other Essays* (New York: Penguin, 1969).
2. From a 1905 edition of *Webster's Dictionary*.
3. See at *www.psychologytoday.com/articles/pto–19981101–000003 .html*.
4. *People* magazine (June 6, 2005), 23.
5. Lionel Tiger, *The Decline of Males: The First Look at an Unexpected New World for Men and Women* (New York: St. Martin's, 2000), in *Publishers Weekly* review (1999).
6. See *No More Christian Nice Guy* (Minneapolis: Bethany House Publishers, 2005) for additional support.
7. Brad Wilcox, *The Importance of Fatherhood for the Healthy Development of Children.* Child Abuse and Neglect User Manual Series. (Washington, DC: U.S. Department of Health and Human Services, 2004).
8. Ibid.
9. Ibid.
10. John Gray, *Men Are From Mars, Women Are From Venus* (New York: HarperCollins Publishers, 1992).
11. *www.parade.com/articles/editions/2006/edition_04-09-2006/Tom_Cruise_cover.*

12. Dr. Laura Schlessinger, *Bad Childhood—Good Life* (New York: HarperCollins Publishers).

13. Ibid, 10.

14. Thomas Lewis, Fari Amini, and Richard Lannon, *A General Theory of Love* (New York: Vintage, 2000), 211.

15. Ibid.

16. See at *www.nationofwimps.com/nationofwimps.php*.

17. Ibid.

18. From a phone interview.

19. Some of the following is quoted or summarized from *No More Christian Nice Guy*.

20. Stu Weber, *The Heart of a Tender Warrior: Becoming a Man of Purpose* (Eugene, OR: Multnomah, 2002).

21. Frederica Mathewes-Green, "God as Suffering Parent." See at *www.beliefnet.com/story/1/story_129_1.html*.

22. Philip Yancey, *The Jesus I Never Knew* (Grand Rapids: Zondervan, 2002).

23. Shmuley Boteach, *Face Your Fear: Living With Courage in an Age of Caution* (New York: St. Martin's Press, 2004), 151.

24. Eugene H. Peterson, *The Message* (Colorado Springs: Navpress, 2002), 647.

25. From personal conversation.

Chapter 3

1. Cited in Gary Thomas, *Sacred Marriage* (Grand Rapids: Zondervan, 2002).

2. Coleman, *The Complete Idiot's Guide to Intimacy*, 148.

3. Gray, *Men Are From Mars*, 45.

4. Ibid., 59.

5. Allender and Longman, *The Intimate Mystery*, 57–58.

6. Ibid., 42.

7. Ibid., 44.

8. Ibid., 59.

9. Ibid., 60.

10. Ibid., 62.

11. Coleman, *Complete Idiot's Guide to Intimacy*, 234–35.

Chapter 4

1. Boteach, *Face Your Fear,* 8.
2. To learn more about how he can overcome fear, see *No More Christian Nice Guy.*
3. From the American Psychological Association; see at *apa.org/releases/ parentalsupport.html.*
4. From article online: "Psychologists Try to Help Men Get Help, Open Up."
5. Gary Thomas, *Sacred Marriage,* 77.
6. Liz Curtis Higgs in *Today's Christian Woman* at *www.christianitytoday .com/tcw/2006/001/5.16html.*
7. Robert and Pamela Crosby, *Creative Conversation Starters for Couples* (Colorado Springs: Honor, 2000).

Chapter 5

1. Fyodor Dostoyevsky, *The Brothers Karamazov* (New York: Bantam, 1984).
2. Coleman, *The Complete Idiot's Guide to Intimacy,* 10.
3. Adapted from Ibid., 120–21.
4. See at *http://www.nationofwimps.com/nationofwimps.php.*
5. Ibid.
6. Op. cit.
7. Nancy Kennedy, "Eight Points That Show, Christian or Not, He's Still a Guy" Focus on the Family Web site: *www.family.org/married/comm/ a001604.cfm.*
8. Coleman, *The Complete Idiot's Guide to Intimacy,* 17.
9. Allender and Longman, *Intimate Mystery,* 77, 79.
10. Ibid., 79.
11. David Schnarch, "Joy With Your Underwear Down," *Psychology Today* (July/August 1994).
12. Ibid.
13. Ibid.
14. Philip Yancey, *Reaching for the Invisible God* (Grand Rapids: Zondervan, 2002).
15. Peterson, *The Message.*

Chapter 6

1. Ernest Hemingway, *A Farewell to Arms* (New York: Scribner, 1995).
2. Lynne Hybels, *Nice Girls Don't Change the World* (Grand Rapids: Zondervan, 2005, 89).
3. Ibid., 91–92.
4. John Stott, *God's New Society* (Downers Grove, IL: InterVarsity Press, 1979), 218–19.
5. Allender and Longman, *Intimate Mystery,* 94.
6. David Murrow, *Why Men Hate Going to Church* (Nashville: Thomas Nelson, 2005). (In conversation with author.)
7. Lewis, Amini, and Lannon, *A General Theory of Love,* 209.
8. Ibid.
9. Blaise Pascal, *Penseés,* trans. A. J. Krailsheimer (New York: Penguin, 1995).

Chapter 7

1. Emerson Eggerichs, *Love & Respect: The Love She Most Desires, the Respect He Desperately Needs* (Franklin, TN: Integrity, 2004), 192.
2. James, Dobson, *Love Must Be Tough* (Sisters, OR: Multnomah, 2004), 196.
3. Angela Thomas in a *New Man* article, n.d.
4. Dobson, *Love Must Be Tough,* 193.
5. Sources: Richard J. Gelles, PhD, "The Missing Persons of Domestic Violence: Male Victims" in *The Women's Quarterly* (Fall 1999); Source: References Examining Assaults by Women on Their Spouses or Male Partners: An Annotated Bibliography by Martin S. Fiebert, Department of Psychology, California State-Long Beach. *www.csulb.edu/mfiebert/assault.htm*; Patricia Pearson, *When She Was Bad: Violent Women & the Myth of Innocence* (New York: Penguin, 1998), 119–123; David Fontes, PsyD, CEAP, "Violent Touch: Breaking Through the Stereotype" at *www.safe4all.org/essays/vtbreak.pdf*; Cathy Young, *Ceasefire! Why Women and Men Must Join Forces to Achieve True Equality* (New York: The Free Press, 1999), 91–96.
6. Philip W. Cook, *Abused Men—The Hidden Side of Domestic Violence* (Westport, CT: Praeger Trade, 1997).
7. Sources: Alan M. Dershowitz, *The Abuse Excuse: And Other Cop-outs,*

Sob Stories and Evasions of Responsibility. (Boston: Little Brown, 1994), 311–13; see the section "Wives Also Kill Husbands—Quite Often" at *www.uiowa.edu/030116/158/articles/dershowitz3.htm*; 1994–95 U.S. Department of Justice Bureau of Justice Statistics Publications Catalog, NCJ 43498, "Murder in Families"; Warren Farrell, *Women Can't Hear What Men Don't Say* (New York: Penguin Putnam, 1999), 150–51.

8. U.S. Department of Health and Human Services, Administration on Children, Youth, and Families, Child Maltreatment 1997: *Reports from the States to the National Child Abuse and Neglect Data System* (Washington, DC: GPO, 1999); *www.acf.dhhs.gov/programs/cb/publications/ncands97/s7.htm*.

9. Eggerichs, *Love & Respect*.

10. Ibid.

11. Ibid.

12. Ibid., 49.

13. John Przybys, "Unfaithfully Yours: Men, Women Have Differing Ideas About Fidelity," *Las Vegas Review-Journal* (March 29, 1998); Jennifer P. Schneider, Richard R. Irons, and M. Deborah Corley, "Disclosure of Extramarital Sexual Activities by Sexually Exploitative Professionals and Other Persons With Addictive or Compulsive Sexual Disorders" in *Journal of Sex Education and Therapy* 24 (1999): 277–87.

14. Dobson, *Love Must Be Tough*.

15. Joan Lunden in *Healthy Living Magazine* as quoted on *www.quotationspage.com/quotes*.

16. Dobson, *Love Must Be Tough*, 199.

Chapter 8

1. Coleman, *The Complete Idiot's Guide to Intimacy*, 69–70. Used with permission.

2. Cecil G. Osborne, *The Art of Understanding Your Mate* (Grand Rapids: Zondervan, 1988), 51–52.

3. Adapted from Coleman, *The Complete Idiot's Guide to Intimacy*, 73.

4. See at *www.nationofwimps.com/nationofwimps.php*.

Chapter 9

1. Hybels, *Nice Girls Don't Change the World.*
2. Lori Gordon, PhD, with Jon Frandsen, *Passage to Intimacy* (Wichita: Fireside, 2001).
3. See at *seattletimes.nwsource.com/html/health/2002820091_healthpleasedisease22.html.*
4. Madame Jeanne Guyon, *Spiritual Torrents* (Sargent, GA: Seedsowers, 1989).
5. Charles R. Swindoll, *Getting Through the Tough Stuff: It's Always Something!* (Nashville: W Publishing Group, 2004), as quoted in *Today's Christian* (March/April 2005), 32.
6. William James, *Varieties of Religious Experience* (Modern Library, 1999).
7. Adapted from Coleman, *The Complete Idiot's Guide to Intimacy,* 62.
8. Ibid.
9. Adapted from Ibid., 114.
10. C. S. Lewis, *Mere Christianity* (San Francisco: HarperSanFrancisco, 2001), chapter 14.
11. Ibid.

Chapter 10

1. Lewis, *Mere Christianity,* chapter 26.
2. Cited in Thomas, *Sacred Marriage.*
3. Kathleen and Thomas Hart, *The First Two Years of Marriage* (Mahwah, NJ: Paulist Press, 1983).
4. Op. cit.
5. Henri J. M. Nouwen, *The Only Necessary Thing* (New York: Crossroad Classic, 1999), 153.
6. C. S. Lewis, *Learning in War-Time.* See Philip Yancey, *What's So Amazing About Grace?*
7. Allender and Longman, *Intimate Mystery,* quoted in Gary Thomas, *Sacred Marriage,* 94.